6 50

Finally — a clear understandable description of shame and guilt. Weaving fairy tales with everyday life examples of shame and its debilitating effects speaks gently to the child in each of us, providing a deeper knowledge. This book helps to name that "what-is-wrong-with-me" part of each of us.

Psychotherapist

Jane Middelton-Moz's finely crafted allegory of Giant, Chameleon and Perfect profoundly touches her reader's innermost beliefs and feelings. In this insightful text Middelton-Moz sensitively takes her readers by the hand and leads them on a journey toward self-love and self-acceptance.

Management Consultant

This book in its entirety is a masterpiece. Jane Middelton-Moz is a gifted clinician, story-teller and teacher.

Therapist

This helpful book offers an understandable way to learn to diminish the emotional hurts of a shame-based childhood. Middelton-Moz shows us the role of compassionate listening as she encourages us to give voice to the hurt and to begin our healing.

High School Teacher

At last, an explanation of shame and guilt written in a way that I can understand as a lay person. Now I have something to work with in my recovery.

Stockbroker

July 1 '92

Melanie Sweetheart

At times the human experience can be wracked with confusion and pain, sorrow and regret.

And sometimes, at the right time, someone can help to make sense of the chaos.

I hope your journey through these pages will open that door; to where sense is replacing chaos.

Love
Denise

Shame And Guilt

The Masters Of Disguise

Jane Middelton-Moz

Health Communications, Inc.
Deerfield Beach, Florida

Jane Middelton-Moz, MS, CCDC
Bellevue, Washington

Library of Congress Cataloging-in-Publication Data

Middelton-Moz, Jane
  Shame and guilt: the masters of disguise / by Jane Middelton-Moz.
    p.   cm.
  Includes bibliographical references (p.   )
  ISBN 1-55874-072-4
  1. Adult children of dysfunctional families — Mental
health.
  2. Shame.   3. Guilt.   I. Title.
RC455.4.F3M53   1990   89-24730
616.85'822—dc20   CIP

©1990 Jane Middelton-Moz
ISBN 1-55874-072-4

Publisher: Health Communications, Inc.
          3201 S.W. 15th Street
          Deerfield Beach, Florida 33442-8124

Dedication

To: My husband, Rudolph I. Moz.
    My sons, Shawn, Jason, Damien and Forrest
      Middelton.
    My stepdaughter, Melinda Moz.
    My brother, Alex E. Ward.
There is no greater wealth than the riches of the heart offered generously through the love, support and warmth of a caring family. If heart gifts could be measured, I would consider myself to be one of the wealthiest individuals on the planet Earth.

To: Mary Carter, Susan Arthur Harris, Elaine Lussier, Kit Wilson and Anna Latimer — five women who I have known at different ages and stages of my life who have offered continual love, care and warmth and "an honest lullaby."

Acknowledgments

This book would not have been possible without the generosity of time, insights, loving support and contributions of many individuals. Their generous support and talents greatly contribute to the substance of this book.

A very deep and special "thank you" goes out to . . .

Jacquie Hope, a valued friend, who gave generously of her time, energy and talents. Jacquie supported me in a hundred ways throughout the writing process.

My brother, Alex Ward, for his laughter, loving support and work on the word processor.

Jason Middelton and Cindy Wescott, two talented creative artists who provided artwork for the book.

My husband, Rudolph Moz, for his incredible support and long hours of clinical input and feedback.

Alex Barker, Ken Carter, Gordon Dickman, Susan Gibson Breda, Jacquie Hope, Susan Irwin, Shawn Middelton, Damien Middelton, Forrest Middelton, Evelyn Mineo, Trish Pearce, Glenna Pinson, and Robin Wehl, for their extremely valuable editorial comments, insights and feedback at different stages in the writing process.

Diane Lout, my office manager, who consistently offers support and laughter and provides structure and order in my daily life.

Pat Huber, for her extremely competent work on the word processor.

Peter Vegso and the staff of Health Communications for providing long hours, talent and creativity in the publishing of this book.

Luann Jarvie, Suzanne Smith and Gary Seidler, for their warmth, loving care and professional support.

Gershen Kaufman, Helen Block Lewis, Helen Lynd, Merle Fossum, Marilyn Mason, John Bowlby, Polly Crisp, Harriet Lerner, Melanie Klein, Janet Woititz, John Bradshaw, Lorie Dwinell and other talented clinicians for their expert clinical knowledge and teachings that have challenged my mind and heart.

Lorie Dwinell, a valued colleague and friend, for her clinical and personal support.

Marie Stilkind, my editor, whose insight, talent, patience and additional support was invaluable to me.

Michael Miller, a talented editor, for his insights, gift with words and consistent help and advice.

A very deep and special thanks to my clients, consultees and the participants in my seminars and workshops, without whose personal knowledge and sharing this book would never have been possible.

An Explanation

The individuals mentioned in the case examples are composites of many adult children whom I have seen in my 23 years of clinical practice . . . individuals who grew up in shaming families and communities. The experiences of being reared in shaming environments are frequently similar. Any similarity of examples to specific individuals is only a result of these common characteristics.

Contents

Introduction

The impact of growing up in a shaming environment affects an individual's life. Debilitating shame affects our ability to form loving relationships, honor ourselves adequately and may impact our future generations. Yet it has only been in the last ten years that the dynamics of shame have received attention in the field of psychology. Helen Block Lewis (1987) in her book, *The Role of Shame in Symptom Formation*, refers to shame as the "sleeper." Earlier attention was focused on guilt and frequently the two emotions were confused. Shame was ignored entirely. It makes sense that shame would be ignored in that it is one of the most difficult feelings to communicate. We are ashamed of our shame.

Books on shame are now being published. This is an important step in bringing it out of hiding. It is my feeling that debilitating shame and guilt are at the root of all dysfunctions in families. Our understanding of these masters of disguise will enhance our understanding of all adult children of dysfunctional families and/or communities. It will help explain why many adult children of depressed parents, abuse, religious fanaticism, war, cultural oppression and parental and sibling death (to name a few) identify so readily with the characteristics of adult children of alcoholics. All these adult children have one thing in common . . . they grew up in shaming environments where the grief of the past was not resolved in the past and their parents in delayed grief could not healthily bond to children.

Some of the difficulties that we have faced in understanding the concepts of debilitating shame and guilt are
that the concepts have been confused historically in the
literature and that the theoretical information has been
difficult to understand.

When I was asked to write a clear easy-to-understand
book on shame and guilt, I was excited by the challenge.
I found that using fairy tales to portray shaming environments allowed readers to reach the shamed child in
themselves and added clarity to sometimes difficult concepts. Throughout my research I found that there were
definable characteristics of shaming environments re-
counted by adult children who experienced debilitating
shame in childhood. In this book characteristics of shame-
based behavior in relationships are explored and defined.
I have listed these characteristics in several sections and
have given examples that I believe will aid in the understanding of each characteristic on an emotional as well as
cognitive level.

As an introduction to the chapters that follow, I list and
describe common characteristics of adults shamed as children and shame-based adults in relationships.

Characteristics Of Adults Shamed In Childhood

1. **Adults shamed as children are afraid of vulnerability and fear exposure of self.**
2. **Adults shamed as children may suffer extreme
   shyness, embarrassment and feelings of being inferior to others. They don't believe they *make* mistakes. Instead they believe they *are* mistakes.**
3. **Adults shamed as children fear intimacy and tend
   to avoid real commitment in relationships. These
   adults frequently express the feeling that one foot
   is out of the door, prepared to run.**
4. **Adults shamed as children may appear either grandiose and self-centered or seem selfless.**

5. Adults shamed as children feel that, "No matter what I do, it won't make a difference; I am and always will be worthless and unlovable."

6. Adults shamed as children frequently feel defensive when even minor negative feedback is given. They suffer feelings of severe humiliation if forced to look at mistakes or imperfections.

7. Adults shamed as children frequently blame others before they can be blamed.

8. Adults shamed as children may suffer from debilitating guilt. These individuals apologize constantly. They assume responsibility for the behavior of those around them.

9. Adults shamed as children feel like outsiders. They feel a pervasive sense of loneliness throughout their lives, even when surrounded with those who love and care.

10. Adults shamed as children project their beliefs about themselves onto others. They engage in mind-reading that is not in their favor, consistently feeling judged by others.

11. Adults shamed as children often feel angry and judgmental towards the qualities in others that they feel ashamed of in themselves. This can lead to shaming others.

12. Adults shamed as children often feel ugly, flawed and imperfect. These feelings regarding self may lead to focus on clothing and makeup in an attempt to hide flaws in personal appearance and self.

13. Adults shamed as children often feel controlled from the outside as well as from within. Normal spontaneous expression is blocked.

14. Adults shamed as children feel they must do things perfectly or not at all. This internalized belief frequently leads to performance anxiety and procrastination.

15. Adults shamed as children experience depression.

16. Adults shamed as children lie to themselves and others.

17. Adults shamed as children block their feelings of shame through compulsive behaviors like workaholism, eating disorders, shopping, substance abuse, list-making or gambling.

18. Adults shamed as children often have caseloads rather than friendships.

19. Adults shamed as children often involve themselves in compulsive processing of past interactions and events and intellectualization as a defense against pain.

20. Adults shamed as children are stuck in dependency or counter-dependency.

21. Adults shamed as children have little sense of emotional boundaries. They feel constantly violated by others. They frequently build false boundaries through walls, rage, pleasing or isolation.

Characteristics Of Shame-Based Adults In Relationships:

1. We lose ourselves in love.

2. When we argue, we fight for our lives.

3. We expend a great deal of energy in mind-reading. We frequently talk to ourselves about what our partners are feeling and needing more than to our partners.

4. We pay a high price for those few good times.

5. We often sign two contracts upon commitment, one conscious and another which is unconscious.

6. We blame and are blamed.

7. We want them gone, then fight to get them back.

8. We know it will be different but expect it to be the same.

9. We often feel that our partners are controlling our behavior.

10. We are frequently attracted to the emotional qualities in another that we have disowned in ourselves.

11. We often create triangles in relationships.

12. We seek the unconditional love from our partners that we didn't receive adequately in a shaming childhood.

Throughout the remainder of this book, these characteristics will be fully explored.

Prologue

Much of what we believe about the world and ourselves is formed in childhood. Parents, those "giants" who take care of us, serve as the mirrors in which we not only create an image of who we are, but how we feel about the person we are becoming.

Childhood can seem like a magical time. We see the world in simple ways, events take place for simple reasons. In a home where the emotional environment is shaped by shaming or guilt-ridden parents, we can come to believe that we are at fault for all of the bad things that happen.

Myths and fairy tales are some of the most powerful sources of life's lessons for children. Stories of whimsy and magical powers, these tales were filled with images of good and evil, right and wrong and portrayals of what good little boys and girls should do and be.

Even as adults, some of our deepest memories, beliefs and attitudes can be traced to the themes of our favorite myths or fairy tales. So as you begin to read this book, you will be taken back to "Once upon a time . . ." to experience a metaphorical tale of a little girl living with parents who tried to love her as best they could.

The Giant
And The Chameleon

Lessons In The Development Of Debilitating Shame

Once upon a time not long ago in the Kingdom of The Universe, there lived Giant and his mate, Chameleon. They lived in a house set high on a hill above a village called The World.

Giant and Chameleon rarely spoke to each other or anyone else, for that matter. Chameleon was very shy and lived, so she believed, only to please Giant. Giant because of his great stature, acted as though he was superior to everyone else, including Chameleon. He seldom spoke to anyone and when he did, it was almost always to correct others, to brag about his generosity, great strength and long list of accomplishments. When others would dare to question him or criticize his bullying behavior, Giant would become enraged. He would remind them of his power and retreat to his space which no one dared enter. Giant was only comfortable completely alone or in total control.

When Chameleon would venture out to the market for groceries, to go to work or to shop, she felt frightened and vulnerable. Unlike Giant, Chameleon felt herself to be less than everyone else in almost every way. Being with others felt embarrassing. She felt proud of Giant and the little pride she had in herself was that he had chosen her for his mate. Without him next to her, she felt worthless and unlovable.

When there was no choice but to be around others, Chameleon would hide inside herself and study them. She watched their gestures, studied their moods, listened attentively to their beliefs and concerns, attempting to fulfill whatever was expected of her. She was very good at becoming what others thought she should be. She held others in awe and feared them.

3

The smallest conflict terrified her, which made her feel even more ashamed that she was afraid. By watching others and looking like the image of their desires, she could become invisible in their presence. Invisibility was her safety; yet she felt angry after she became invisible. She often found herself mulling over these interactions long after a brief meeting.

Sometimes in the evening she would talk to Giant about the people she had met. Together they would judge the others' weaknesses. Giant relished these times of lecturing and criticizing the "others" with Chameleon. Chameleon only felt guilty for her behavior. She needed to speak of their good points. These discussions always seemed to bring Giant closer to her in a way he rarely was. It was clear he felt they were better than others, as if it were the two of them against "The World."

It terrified Chameleon that Giant would someday see that she was more unlovable and flawed than any of those they relished in judging. She always took great pains to hide her tail, but she knew he must somehow see only her tail and wonder why he had chosen her.

Giant didn't want children, feeling they would interrupt the life he had grown quite fond of. He had taken good care of Chameleon, protected her and, in return, she had worshiped him. He had given her everything.

"Why do you need a child?" he would ask. "Am I not enough?"

But, alas, Chameleon's pleas only became more desperate. She begged Giant repeatedly to grant her this one desire. But he would walk away and she would dissolve into sobs.

Her tears pulled at a place in him that Giant hadn't felt since childhood, a place only his mother had exposed, a place that frightened him. He eventually agreed to let her have a child.

The first and only child Giant and Chameleon had was born in the winter. Chameleon was overjoyed. As she gazed upon her child, she felt intense pride. She knew her daughter would be strong, beautiful, talented, intelligent; everything Chameleon had only dreamed of being.

She examined her newborn daughter carefully. She saw no flaws, and most importantly, no tail. She knew her daughter would not be imperfect like she was. Chameleon tried to remember whether she had had a tail at birth or if it and her coloring had developed later. She couldn't remember. But she was satisfied that her precious daughter would become a giant even more grand than her mate and her mother had been.

She named the child after her mother and Giant's grandmother. Her name was to be Perfect Giant.

This beautiful little child would soon become the companion she had always wanted. She would be someone to talk to, someone to love her unconditionally in the way that no one, including her own family, ever had. Perfect would never be the disappointment Chameleon had been to her own mother. Her daughter would admire her and give her respect. At last Chameleon would be the center of someone's world. In return Chameleon would give Perfect everything.

Perfect occupied all of Chameleon's time. Giant became more and more depressed. Mysteriously, he started getting smaller.

"She doesn't need me any longer," he thought. "I'm no longer the center of her world." So he would stay locked in his room day and night.

Soon Giant and Chameleon weren't talking at all. Although she felt a bit rejected, Chameleon never asked Giant questions, fearing he would leave her or demand time that was now devoted to Perfect. She knew he could take care of himself. Besides her baby girl needed her and Perfect met her needs for companionship more than Giant ever had.

Chameleon slept in Perfect's room. She would talk to her daughter while she slept, telling her all about her sorrows. When Perfect woke, she would gaze intently into her mother's eyes. For the first time, Chameleon was the center of another's world. Her tail no longer bothered her. It seemed to be disappearing.

When Perfect would cry, Chameleon felt irritated, but eventually would laugh at her child's tears. "You have no reason to cry, silly girl. You are strong, tough, beautiful and gifted. I give you everything I have and more. Don't you realize that you can't possibly have needs that aren't being fulfilled?"

As the years passed, Giant just kept shrinking while Chameleon's tail seemed to vanish altogether, and Perfect, with only a few stumbling blocks here and there, met all of her mother's expectations for her. When any signs of weakness appeared in her child, Chameleon would either cry or laugh at her daughter's imagined needs or fears and, like magic, the unwanted emotions vanished.

Perfect grew into the exquisitely beautiful giant her mother had imagined. She paid great attention to her body and its shape. She studied diligently. She listened to her mother's troubles day and night, let her mother select her friends from only the very best giants and entertained her mother with great charm. Perfect never left home without making certain first that she looked her best.

Perfect had learned early how dependent Chameleon was on her. She loved her mother, and it pained her to see her mother's reaction when she somehow would disappoint her. When upset, Chameleon would dissolve into sobs and seemed to shrink, getting smaller and smaller.

"After all," Perfect often thought, when her mother's demands tired her, "she has given me her whole life." Perfect even bought her mother roses on her own birthday to thank her for her very birth.

Perfect rarely saw her father. He hid most of the time in his den. Chameleon warned her daughter not to bother her father because she could see he had turned into a dragon. Sometimes, however, Perfect's curiosity would get the best of her and she'd enter her father's den. Most of the time Giant would be extremely irritable and his temper would frighten Perfect. But sometimes Giant looked small and very, very sad.

Once when she was still young but already large in stature, Perfect worked day and night on a gift for her father. She had learned that in his happier days he had loved horses, so she now set out to carve him a miniature horse out of wood. She spent hours on a perfect mane and tail and when she finished, she painted it black.

She remembered stories her mother had told her that the horse represented freedom, and black stallions were the proudest of them all. She even wrapped the treasure in paper she had painted herself. She carried it carefully to her father, making sure he was awake so she wouldn't disturb him unnecessarily.

Giant took the package, tore off the wrapping, then looked at her in amazement.

"What in the world is this thing?" he laughed uncomfortably. "It's not my birthday, you know. Here, take it back. Give it to me again on my birthday." Perfect heard him laughing as she ran to her room.

When she was older, Perfect discovered that the one thing that would really please her father was to listen to his stories. He would tell her again and again of his past accomplishments, expound on his generosity and lecture her endlessly on the lessons life taught. For those brief periods of time, her father would be his giant self again and the fire-breathing dragon he had become would disappear.

She would listen in a daze until sometimes she almost fell asleep. Sometimes it seemed he was talking to someone else. He was no longer aware of her, but it felt good just to be with him.

He never mentioned the horse again and neither did she. She told herself how silly it had been to give her father the homemade thing. After all, he was worldly. She felt ashamed of herself for her past childishness. For she was a giant and should have known better. She felt very embarrassed whenever she appeared to be stupid.

One spring day, at the end of her last year of school, Perfect's world seemed to come to an abrupt stop. She had been eating very little the entire week before and had been particularly tired and confused. She had taken her final exam in her best subject. Now she sat frozen in her seat as the failing grade stared almost accusingly up at her. Quick calculations told her that she could not receive high marks for the term. Mediocre, she thought, shocked and terrified. She had never been mediocre before. Her mother would fall apart. Her father would scream.

The last bell had barely rung before Perfect was out of her seat. She ran and ran, not caring where. She briefly thought of suicide, but realized it would kill her mother. She felt herself becoming smaller and smaller. All she had been given had been a waste. How could anyone tolerate "average?" No giant would want her, not that she had an interest in anyone. Her whole life centered on pleasing her mother and doing her studies.

Perfect ran deep into the woods until she could run no more. She lay down on the grass and cried and cried. She tried to stop, but couldn't. Giants didn't cry. Giants were strong. Giants were superior. Her shame grew while she continued to shrink. "I've never been strong. I've always been stupid and weak," she cried.

"Can I help you in some way?"

The voice seemed to come out of nowhere.

"Who are you?" Perfect stuttered, wanting to fall right through the earth. It was bad enough that a giant was weeping but now someone was seeing her weakness. She felt herself turn color and could sense a tail beginning to grow where none had ever been.

"I'm a human being," the voice answered. "You seemed to be in trouble and I wanted to know if you needed help."

Perfect had only heard of human beings, but never known one. Her father said they were a much lower form of life. Although she had feared them in days gone by, her mother feared them less than giants. Humans were mostly average and had no ambitions to move to the high places. Perfect had sometimes watched them from her high place. They played and sang . . . laughed and cried openly. She saw them touching each other and sometimes getting angry. They appeared to her almost shameless. She was jealous of them at times, then was ashamed of her jealousy. After all, she was a giant — although at that moment she didn't feel like one.

"I can't let you see me like this," Perfect muttered. "I've . . . I've been crying. I look terrible. My eyes are red and . . . and," she searched for words as she carefully hid her tail, "I'm not up to visitors." She crawled further into the taller grass until she became invisible.

"No one should have to be alone when they're sad," Human Being replied. "I haven't noticed anything wrong with your appearance or clothing. You look fine as you are."

"I do?" Perfect whispered. She had been told often that she was a beauty — tough, silly, stupid, selfish and, at times, fat, but never fine the way she was.

"Of course, you do. Do you need to look a particular way to be comforted when you're sad?"

"I'm not supposed to be sad," Perfect said. "Giants are never sad."

"Giants?" Human Being questioned. "You're not a giant."

"I'm not?" Perfect queried sadly. She began to feel smaller. She realized that her color was changing and that must mean her tail was growing longer. "I must have turned into a chameleon," she said to herself. "Mother will be devastated. Father will be enraged."

"You're a human being like everyone else," Human Being replied, wondering what she had meant by her statement. He had heard some of those who lived in High Places thought they were different, better than others. Perhaps she was one of them.

"A human being!" she cried.

"Of course, you are! All of us who live in The World are human beings. I've heard stories about giants, but I've never seen one. Certainly you don't think you're a giant? You look just like me. See for yourself. There is a pool not far behind you. Look at your reflection."

Perfect crawled deeper into the tall grass until she came to a clearing that surrounded a small clear pond. She carefully crawled to the edge and looked into the water. There before her she saw the reflection of a young woman. It was definitely a human being who stared back at her.

"Do you see?" Perfect heard the voice call. "Come on out, let me see you. I won't hurt you. Let's just talk a while."

"Are you trying to trick me?" Perfect asked, crawling back to her place in the grass, still afraid to come out.

"No, of course not," Human Being replied. "I've known others who have come to this place, thinking they were something else. One fellow thought he was a rat, another a pig and another a mouse. All were human beings."

"But, I've looked in mirrors. I've never seen myself like this."

"Most mirrors only reflect back what you think yourself to be. The pool of water that you just looked into is the Pond of Clarity. It shows you as you are. Most are afraid to look; they are afraid to see. It's a shock to change perceptions."

Perfect felt enraged. "Why have my parents not told me? Why have they insisted that I was a giant? Why do they lie? I hate them!" Almost as fast as the words left her mouth, Perfect felt overwhelming guilt, then almost as quickly, felt small again.

"I can understand your anger," Human Being said, "but I'm sure they only saw you as they needed you to be, perhaps as they saw themselves to be. The World is a strange place sometimes. I'm sorry you've been hurt. You know, not far from here is another pond that might help. It's called The Pond of Timelessness and I've heard that it has helped many others. Please let me take you there."

Perfect climbed out of the tall grass and stood next to Human Being. She looked down and could feel her coloring. "I'm so ashamed," she said quietly. "I feel so stupid and I don't know why."

"Perhaps we can find out why together," Human Being said softly, aware of Perfect's embarrassment. "Perhaps it will be easier if you can keep telling yourself that you're a human being, no more, no less. We make mistakes, we're not perfect."

"I am," Perfect laughed for the first time. "That's my name — Perfect."

"What?"

"Never mind. How do we get to this place?"

"It's just up the road. Come on, we'll be there in no time."

As they walked, they shared about their lives. Perfect began to feel a trust in Human Being she had never felt before in anyone. A warmth grew in the center of her being.

"I did poorly on a test today," she said bravely, feeling the color grow and hating it.

"Is that a problem for you?"

"Well, I thought it was."

"Was it a subject that you usually do well in? Is it your favorite class?"

"I usually do well in everything. I've never known what I liked or what I didn't. I've never thought about it. I was just busy doing things well. It's odd to think of liking something."

"Look," Human Being interrupted, "there's the pond."

As they got closer, Perfect felt a strange sense of fear. She wanted to run.

"Don't worry," Human Being said softly, gently taking Perfect's hand and leading her to the edge of the pond. "Many feel a little frightened here. It's difficult to see things as they are sometimes. Change can be very frightening. I'll be sitting right here with you."

"What should I do?"

"The Pond of Timelessness has stored within its depths, images of our lives. As you look into the pond, think back to your childhood. It will reflect back to you memories that have supported your beliefs in yourself."

"Will you see the images too?" Perfect asked, feeling frightened again as color flushed her face.

"Only if you wish to share them," Human Being replied, understanding Perfect's shame.

As Perfect stared into the water, she began to see an image of herself as a little girl. She was standing outside her house. It was wintertime. She realized it was her birthday. She appeared to be three or four years old. The snow was very deep and the little girl stood crying. The small child was stuck, buried past her waist in snow. Perfect abruptly turned away from the scene in front of her.

"What a stupid kid," Perfect cried. "She could never do anything right. I remember that day so well. Looking at it makes me feel the same as I did when I looked at my test paper today. I hate her so. She was always so clumsy. Look there, the stupid kid's stuck in the snow. She's acting like a baby!"

Human Being looked into the water, "You were young and frightened. You were cold and hurting. Why isn't someone helping you? Why would anyone let a child suffer so? Where's your mother or your father?"

Perfect looked again into the water and saw her mother standing close by the child taking her picture and laughing. She saw her father angrily looking down from the upstairs window.

"Why was she taking a picture when you were in such pain?" Human Being asked. "You must have been very frightened."

Perfect felt a pain growing within her and began to cry. She hid her face as she turned away from the scene in front of her. "I don't know why I'm crying. I'm sorry. You mustn't see me like this."

"Don't apologize for your tears," Human Being said, gently touching Perfect's shoulder. "You're crying because that child you were seems so alone and frightened."

"Why doesn't she just get out of there instead of being such a cry baby? She's so stupid!"

"She's a little child. She's stuck. She can't move. She's stuck and needs help. Why didn't someone help you instead of laughing at your pain?"

For the first time, Perfect looked and saw herself as a child. She had never thought of herself as a child. She felt the child's pain and realized that her tears were for the child's loneliness. She felt what it was truly like for the little girl she really was and for the first time her shame seemed to dissolve.

"I was never a giant," she cried. "I was just a little girl, a human being."

Perfect came back many times to The Pond of Time-lessness in the months that followed. Human Being always sat by her as she saw more and more images reflected in the pond's clear waters. She began to feel stronger, neither a giant nor a chameleon but very human. She began to like being a human being. As time passed, she enjoyed her friend's kindness and touch. She began crying without hiding her face or turning color. She laughed more and learned to play.

One day she decided it was time to join the human beings.

"I've decided I no longer want to live in the High Places," Perfect said one afternoon. "It's sad leaving Mother and Father, but it no longer feels comfortable to live as a Giant or a Chameleon. I have tried so hard to get them to come with me to the Pond of Clarity. I think they are afraid. I'm not angry at them anymore. They believe they are not Human. I can't change that. I wish I could. Can I go with you today instead of going back to the High Places?"

"Of course you can," Human Being said happily. "We can ride there together," he said pointing in the direction of the field.

As they turned to go, Perfect saw a black stallion grazing in the tall grasses. She thought sadly of the mini-ature horse she had carved for her father so many years before. She realized why he had loved horses in his youth. And why now he feared them so.

Perfect joined the human beings and lived contentedly ever after. Giant came out of his room and once again took care of Chameleon and they lived as they always had — in the High Places.

Years before Giant had rescued the miniature horse that Perfect had thought was gone forever. He never let anyone know he had it, but would look at it longingly on rainy days. At those times Giant vaguely recalled a time when he thought that perhaps he, too, had been a human being. The thought frightened him. He felt at these times a strange mixture of longing, envy, disgust and, finally, a sense of shame deep inside. He would quickly hide the horse behind several loose stones in his study wall. He hid the shame of what the horse represented from Chameleon and, more importantly, from himself.

Debilitating Shame: What Is It?

Shame is a feeling deep within our being that makes us want to hide, as Perfect did in the tall grasses. We feel suddenly overwhelmed and self-conscious. The feeling of shame is of being exposed, visible and examined by a critical other. It is the sense that the "examination" has found the self to be imperfect and unworthy in every way. We hang our heads, stoop our shoulders and curve inward as if trying to make ourselves invisible.

Who is the critical other from whom we are hiding? In Perfect's case, it was the eyes and voice of Chameleon that were now her own internal judge and jury.

She lay down on the grass and cried. She tried and tried to stop but couldn't. Giants didn't cry. Giants were strong. Giants were superior. Her shame grew and she continued to shrink.

Perfect's shame grew in proportion to her awareness that she had not lived up to her mother's ideal that she was to be a giant, which had become Perfect's fantasy ideal of herself. Perfect's awareness of her own tears meant that she was not a giant and, since Chameleon could only love giants, she was not worthy of love. When we experience shame, our eyes turn inward on ourselves. Shame is the experience of the self judging who we are against the image that significant adults in our childhood have given us through their actions, words and gestures. When we feel shame, we see ourselves having failed to live up to that fantasy image created for us.

As stated by Helen Merrell Lynd, "Shame is the outcome, not only of exposing oneself to another person, but of the exposure of oneself to parts of the self that one has not recognized and whose existence one is reluctant to admit." (Lynd, 1961, p. 31)

Shame shows itself in many forms generationally. Parents who suffer from debilitating shame frequently create children, such as Perfect, who also suffer from debilitating shame.

Perfect may have had a sister, Imperfect. Just as Perfect was Chameleon's ideal self, Imperfect may have been the vessel for all of Chameleon and Giant's unwanted qualities. This daughter, or son, unlike Perfect, would see through her parents' eyes, words and gestures that she was a constant failure and disappointment. Nothing she could do would be right.

Imperfect might become too fearful to attempt Chameleon's standards because she would have learned that she could never succeed. She might become frozen with fear and fail in performance or rebel, acting out Chameleon's unexpressed anger at herself. Yet, in a sense, she would always be rewarded for her failure through negative attention. Or Chameleon might see herself in her daughter and become alternately overprotective and angry when Imperfect failed. Imperfect may learn that failure to meet other's expectations may bring attention and nurturing. She might incorporate this into her adult self and equate success with lack of attention or abandonment.

When we experience guilt, the anxiety we feel relates to the fear of punishment. When we feel guilty, we blame our behavior or lack of behavior in a given instance. When we feel shame, it is our self that is being judged. The anxiety we experience in shame relates to the fear of potential isolation and abandonment. If we do not meet the expectations of valued others we risk their rejection. As children, we depend on those valued others for life support. What we unconsciously believe is at risk in a shameful experience is our connectedness to others in our world.

Helen Block Lewis suggests that shame is an emergency response to threatened affectional ties. She further states, "Because shame is the self's vicarious experience of the other's negative evaluation, in order for shame to occur, there must be a relationship between the self and the

other in which the self cares about the other's evaluation."
(Lewis, 1987, p. 16)

We all have had the experience at one time or another,
of not living up to our image of ourselves. We have all,
therefore, experienced shame.

Imagine, for instance, walking into a party dressed in
an elaborate costume. You thought because it is Hallow-
een that the party you've been invited to was a costume
party. When you arrive dressed in the ape costume you
spent weeks working on, you discover that everyone else
is wearing evening gowns and tuxedos. You feel all eyes
upon you. You feel hot in the face and aware of your
every motion. You turn bright red and hope that you can
quickly disappear, but your legs won't move.

What would make this situation more comfortable?
You could begin to laugh and everyone could laugh with
you, thus repairing the interpersonal bridge between yourself and others. Or perhaps, two people who are also
wearing costumes come from across the room to stand
with you. Now you belong. Or perhaps your host or
hostess comes over to you and apologizes for the misun-
derstanding, explaining that they weren't clear in their
invitation. You are no longer isolated. If you laugh and no
one laughs with you . . . if your host or hostess gives you
a look of disgust . . . if everyone stares and says nothing,
shame increases proportionally to your sense of isolation.

We have all experienced shame. But not all have experienced the debilitating shame that caused Perfect to run
away and consider ending her life rather than face the
possibility of being average. It wasn't punishment that
Perfect feared — it was rejection and abandonment. The
judge inside her was harsh and critical. "How could anyone
tolerate average? No giant would want her."

Debilitating shame is an isolating experience that makes
us think we are completely alone and unique in our unlov-
ability. It is a feeling that we are intensely and profoundly
unlovable. Debilitating shame is a state of self-hate and
self-devaluation that is comparable to little else. It makes

us feel that life is happening to us and that we are helpless in the wake of that happening.

When we experience debilitating shame, all reality perspective is lost and we feel that all of our vulnerabilities become exposed and magnified. We believe that others in our world view us with disdain and/or disgust. We think that perhaps we can be accepted if we can only become more lovable or perfect. This often lends us to direct all of our actions towards accomplishing these eluded goals. We no longer feel the temporary shame of having made a mistake in public, or of having momentarily failed an expectation we have set for ourselves. Instead, we *are* mistakes and failures. We are unique and become, or sometimes remain, isolated by that uniqueness.

What Is Pride?

Pride is often considered the opposite of shame. Shame is our failure to live up to the image significant others have expected of us and, thus, we have expected of ourselves. When we feel pride, we have reached "other," then self-related expectations. Both pride and shame are originally "other" related. If we are alone when we experience shame or pride, it is our fantasy of the "other's" eyes on us that direct our own eyes inward. However, if pride is the flip side of shame, then grandiosity is the flip side of debilitating shame.

Chameleon expressed "pride" in Perfect, and thus in herself as Perfect's mother. In order to feel pride, however, Perfect was expected to make up for Chameleon's believed failings. She was to be a giant in every sense of the word. In order, therefore, for Perfect to feel pride in herself, she had to have unrealistic notions of her abilities and importance. Perfect attempted to live up to the impossible image Chameleon dictated. When she failed to meet the image required of her, Perfect felt totally worthless and unlovable (debilitating shame). In order for Perfect to succeed, she had to feel better than anyone else (grandiosity). She could succeed in meeting her expectations of self only if she could succeed in becoming better than others. She had to win over others . . . be stronger . . . be more lovable. She had to be neither a chameleon nor a human being. She could only feel pride if she could be seen, and thus see herself, as a giant.

How Is Debilitating Shame Created In Children?

Many years ago when thinking about shame, I recalled a memory of myself in second grade. I was on my way out for recess when Mrs. Graves, my second grade teacher, called me back. I walked towards her, giving her my brightest smile. She kneeled down beside me, and gently touched me on the shoulders.

"Jane," she said in a loving voice, "you always appear to be such a happy little girl. You are always smiling when I look at you. I wonder though if you are really as happy inside as you seem. Sometimes I think you are unhappy inside." I remember feeling frozen, my face getting hotter and hotter. I recall staring at the floor.

"You are a wonderful little girl," Mrs. Graves continued. "I just want you to know that if something is bothering you, you can always come to me and talk about it. Okay?" I just mumbled, "Okay."

I got out of the room as fast as my legs would carry me. I never forgot that seemingly small interaction. I realized that Mrs. Graves was the first person to attempt to intercede in my debilitating shame. I realize that while standing in front of her, I felt tremendous shame for being unhappy; the shame of feeling shame. She had seen my unhappiness and in seeing it, had made me see it as well.

Like Perfect, I was a child ashamed of feeling unhappiness. I was ashamed of tears, of being sick, of making a mistake or of having needs. Additionally I was ashamed of feeling pride in myself. After recalling the memory, I questioned, why would a six-year-old feel such debilitating shame?

Almost immediately, after asking myself the question, I began to remember my parents' words . . . "Oh, look at the cry baby! Who do you think you are, anyway? . . . You think you're unhappy! What do you think I feel after all I've given you! . . . Look, Little Miss Know-it-all! . . . Pretending to be sick will get you nowhere. . . . Can't you do anything right? . . . Do I have to do everything myself? . . . Oh, it's you. What do you want now?"

Words flooded back into my consciousness and so did the memories of disgusted, angry or laughing faces. I recalled memories of times when my father had experienced shame when I was with him. No words were spoken between us, but I remember feeling shame with him when we were with educated people. His shame eventually became my own. I then realized that shame could be contagious. I remembered feeling shame in elementary school, particularly at holiday times, when teachers would read books about "normal" happy families. I also remembered feeling acute shame on one occasion when I was with my mother and heard her lying to someone about herself.

By recalling incident after incident of shame in my life, I realized that it had been the unresolved, unspoken and repetitive shaming in my young life that had created debilitating shame in me throughout my developmental years. With each incident of shaming, I felt more unlovable, insignificant, isolated and dependent. I realized that the more these shameful experiences were repeated without resolution, the less trusting of myself, and therefore of others, I became. Over time, I felt less sure of the world in which I lived and of my place in that world.

Through remembering and recording memories of shame experiences in my childhood and listening to reports of shameful memories of others, I came to the realization that shame comes in many forms and is directed towards the self in countless verbal and nonverbal ways. I realized that when shameful experiences are repetitive and there is no opportunity to talk about them, the individual feels increasingly more disconnected from her or his world. A sense of internal isolation and uniqueness is the fabric out of which debilitating shame is created.

How Were We Shamed As Children?

The following are examples of interactions between children and their adult caretakers that can result in feelings of shame in children.

1. A child may experience shame when parents and other adult caretakers indicate through their words and/or behaviors that a child is not wanted. This message may be delivered as early as infancy by the way the infant is held and interacted with by the adult caretaker.
2. When a child is humiliated in public, the shame response in the child increases.
3. When disapproval is shown toward the child that is aimed at the child's entire being rather than at a particular behavior.
   Example: "You are a very bad boy," rather than, "Tommy, I don't like it when you hit your sister. I can understand your frustration with her, but I don't want you to hit her again."
4. When a child must hide a part of her or his being in order to be accepted, shame is created in the child.
   Examples: mistakes, needs, joys, sorrows, illness, successes, tears.
5. When a child's emotional or physical boundaries are violated, as occurs in physical or sexual abuse of an overt or covert nature, shame is created in the child. A child cannot develop his or her identity unless clear boundaries exist between parent and child. Physical and sexual abuse from others in the child's environment lead to a sense that, "I am not lovable or accepted . . . I am only lovable and accepted when . . ." The child also grows up in a world of secrets, feeling that, "I must hide myself constantly from the eyes of others."

6. When children feel that they have no privacy, no place to hide, the child grows up with a pervasive sense of inadequacy and thinks, "I must really be a bad person."

   Examples: Parents who go through their children's things, listen in on phone calls, read their mail or make such statements as, "I know what you're thinking . . . If you loved me, you'd tell me everything."

7. When adults ignore or treat indifferently events or gifts that are important to the child, the child feels intense shame.

   Examples: A child works all day on a drawing for mother. Mother doesn't take the time to look at it, hides it away on top of a pile of things or says, "What am I supposed to do with this?" When parents consistently do not attend functions that are important to the child, like ball games, parent-child dinners, or plays, the child develops a sense that he or she is just not important enough.

8. When a child feels by comparison that his parents are somehow different from other powerful figures in the child's world outside the home, the child may begin to feel shame regarding the family, and thus shame of self. This feeling of difference sometimes leads to split loyalties in the child between home and the world outside. This causes the child to hide one part of his world, and thus himself, from the other.

   Examples: Children of immigrant parents whose speech and customs differ from the world outside the home. Children of racial minorities where color has come to mean badness, laziness, powerlessness or helplessness in the world outside the home. Children of poverty, where having lack of money or things is judged to mean nonacceptance.

9. When a child feels that parents or members of the family are somehow flawed, when compared to other adult figures in his or her world, shame develops in the child.

Example: Children where a family member is alcoholic or a drug abuser and their behavior is embarrassing . . . Children where a family member has a physical or mental disability and that difference is never discussed or the child can't express feelings of embarrassment.

10. When trust in important adult figures is damaged or destroyed through inconsistency or neglect, the child experiences confusion about, "Where I belong or what I can expect" from the world. This feeling of disconnectedness or lack of attachment leads to increased internal shame and isolation.

11. When a child grows up with adults who are ashamed and feel powerless in the world, the child also develops a sense of shame. Shame is contagious.

12. When a child is made to feel unwanted, unlovable, flawed or worthless in the broader world of school or community, debilitating shame develops in that child.

    Example: Children who have difficulty learning to read because of undetected learning disabilities and through words or behaviors are made to feel lazy or stupid. Through neglect at home, children who come to school inappropriately dressed or with poor hygiene are isolated, made fun of or looked at with disgust by those in the world of school and community. Some children are treated with sympathy by well-meaning adults who increase their sense of insecurity, lack of self-respect and powerlessness in the outside world.

13. When a child is consistently blamed for the actions or emotional state of their adult caretakers and there is no way that the child can understand what is expected, let alone fulfill the expectations, both debilitating shame and debilitating guilt develop. The child feels, "If only I were smarter, stronger, more lovable, then my parents would drink less, be happier or less depressed."

14. When a child cannot live up to the expectations of the adult caretakers because their expectations are inconsistent or unrealistic given the child's developmental capabilities or humanness, the child feels like Perfect did, worthless, not lovable, a failure, a mistake. Debilitating shame is thus created and perpetuated.

15. When parents or adult caretakers use silent disgust as a way of disciplining a child's behavior, the child feels that their entire being is bad. When silent rejection is used as punishment, there is little opportunity for the child to repair the relationship. The child is left with both irreparable guilt for the behavior and debilitating shame.

    Example: Tommy brings home a note from school saying he was in a fight during recess. Later that evening Tommy shows the note to his parents. They read the note and look at Tommy with disgust. Sighing, they put the note face down on the table. Tommy's parents walk off, leaving him alone in the room. The infraction at school is never discussed. There is no closure.

2

A Master Of Disguises

Characteristics Of Adults Shamed In Childhood

Just as in the story of Chameleon and Giant, many myths, fairy tales and fables exemplify the hidden dynamics of shame in their characters. In *The Wizard of Oz* (Baum, 1936) everyone sought the Great and Powerful Oz. Indeed an entire kingdom was built on his reputation. Originally the Tin Man, Lion, Scarecrow and Dorothy stood in awe of his power, cowering before his booming voice, magical appearance and fierce demands. When, however, a tiny dog stripped the Great and Powerful Oz of his disguise, it was Oz who cowered. Stripped of his disguise, Oz was self-conscious, frightened, timid, apologetic and insecure. Oz felt ashamed that he could not exercise the magical power of which even he had come to believe himself capable.

In *Snow White and the Seven Dwarfs* (Walt Disney Productions, 1937), Snow White's stepmother, the Wicked Queen, lacked self-esteem. She stood before a mirror daily in order to assure herself of her worthiness and personal power, just as many parents who are lacking self-esteem demand unwavering reverence by their children. It is only in their children's mirroring that they can feel self-worth. When the queen's mirror would not reflect her as the "fairest of them all," she hid her injury and shame behind a wall of rage and fantasies of revenge. Snow White, of course, after receiving internal wounds from her stepmother's food, could only be brought back to life through the love of a handsome prince.

Even the Seven Dwarfs appeared to be symbolic of the "false selves" (disguises) we must hide behind. They reflected the parts of ourselves we must disown in order to find nurturing and acceptance. Sneezy was always sick. Happy was joyful from morning until night, while Grumpy, until nurtured, was of course, grumpy. Doc intellectual-ized everything, while Dopey could not allow himself to believe he had an intelligent thought. Sleepy appeared severely depressed and lethargic and Bashful, until moth-ered by Snow White, showed what we might have recog-nized as the frontal face of shame.

Master Of Disguises

Helen Block Lewis considers shame the *"affective-cognitive state of low self-esteem"* (Lewis, p. 39). Shame is a master of disguises. In Chapter One, both Chameleon and Giant represent faces of shame.

Like Giant, some children whose self-esteem is severely wounded defend against further injury by repressing, deny-ing or disassociating from their shameful feelings. As adults, these children will grow into what appears to be self-centeredness like Giant. They have cloaked themselves in "false pride." They have unrealistic notions of their importance, power and abilities, and frequently see others as weak, less intelligent, needy or defective in order to de-fend themselves against facing their own perceived flaws.

Other children, like Chameleon, will consistently expe-rience intense feelings of shame. These children, as adults, defend themselves by repressing feelings of personal power. They attack themselves before they can be at-tacked by others. They idealize and place in others the feelings of power they fear in themselves.

Although Giant appeared to be egotistical, powerful and self-involved, his behavior can be viewed as the flip side of Chameleon's defense much like the inside and outside of a reversible disguise. Both gave to the other that which they most feared in themselves. Both disguises were sewn from the fabric of painful childhood wounds and debilitating shame.

Perfect's shame was dressed in yet another disguise. In an attempt to defend against the shame of being unable to reach the unrealistic expectations that Chameleon set for her, and to compensate for her defects, Perfect set out on a quest for perfection. This attempt to be perfect, of course, failed because perfection is unattainable. The more she attempted perfection, the more she was doomed to face failure and therefore, more debilitating shame. No matter how well she did, it wasn't good enough. She fiercely judged herself against ever-increasing personal standards and external measurements.

Because she felt inadequate and worthless, nothing she could do would ever be good enough. She couldn't make up for the fact that she wasn't the giant in the mirror of her mother's eye. The more she strove to reduce shame, the more she was overtaken by it. The race couldn't be won. Unfortunately, the disguise of perfection is convincing. Most children, like Perfect, or the adults they have become, rarely get the necessary feedback required to release them from the double binds inherent in their masks.

Survival Mask

When a child is wounded and suffers debilitating shame, the only way they can survive is to defend and adapt to the requirements and needs of those they depend upon for survival. Children, therefore, develop defensive patterns that become rigid and inflexible by adulthood.

Imagine an orange on a tree in the middle of a clearing. It is not yet ripe so it clings, relying on the roots of the tree for nourishment. Perhaps there is a rain storm, then freezing rain. A hail storm develops. In order to protect its center core from the harshness of the environment, the orange grows an increasingly thicker skin for protection. The small child, unable to protect itself, clings to the caretaker. The child must develop a false self, or external disguise, to protect its real self from the harshness of a shaming environment. The following is a list of many characteristics that might be seen in adults who were shamed in childhood.

1. Adults shamed as children are afraid of vulnerability and fear exposure of self.

When Mary met Ted, she had developed a pattern of pleasing others in order to remain invisible. Ted was a leader and a talker. On their first date Ted asked Mary what kind of food she liked. Her response was, for her, a common one, "I don't care . . . it doesn't matter to me . . . you decide." The same response was given when selecting a movie. They ended up eating lobster in a quiet little restaurant on the ocean. Later they saw a thriller at the drive-in. Ted talked all evening about his work and later about the movie. Their future dates followed this pattern.

When they became engaged, Ted planned the wedding, Mary saying, "It doesn't matter to me. What would you like?" Three years later, in their first marital therapy session, Mary complained of Ted's domineering behavior. She used their first date as an example: "We ate lobster . . . I hate fish! We went to a horror movie . . . I hate thrillers!" Ted complained of Mary's dependency. "You always make me make all the decisions. I get sick and tired of deciding everything!" Each realized they knew very little about the other. Neither exposed the most vulnerable parts of themselves to the other or even to themselves. Mary remained invisible behind a wall of "I don't care." Ted hid behind a wall of words and caretaking behavior.

2. Adults shamed as children may suffer extreme shyness, embarrassment and feelings of being inferior to others. They don't believe they *make* mistakes. Instead, they believe they *are* mistakes.

Martha had just been offered a new position at work. The change in job meant a great deal more money and more fringe benefits. Martha's supervisor told her she has been surprised that Martha had neither asked for a higher position nor a merit increase during her five years of outstanding performance. "Your talents could have been permanently hidden. Why didn't you step forward?"

Martha considered turning the new job down because it meant more visibility. "I'm much more comfortable being a behind-the-scenes person. It sometimes frustrates me, however, when I see others taking credit for my work. I'm terrified of attention. When I was a kid in school, I'd rather get an *F* than stand in front of the class and read a report. My face always turned red and I couldn't speak! I wanted to die every time a teacher called on me. I felt like an open book that everyone could read."

When I asked Martha what being visible had meant in her family, she quickly replied, "Being stupid; being bad."

She reported many incidents of being shamed by her mother in front of her brothers and sisters. "Then my face would turn red, and everyone would laugh. I was so ashamed of being ashamed. I'd rather never get a raise than go through that again."

3. Adults shamed as children fear intimacy and tend to avoid real commitment in relationships. There is often a feeling that one foot is already out of the door, prepared to run. This dynamic leads to relationship patterns where one leaves rather than being left, the development of triangles (including affairs), attraction only to those who are unavailable or create psychological distancing through daydreaming or workaholism.

When I was in my late 20s, I remember being shocked when a friend said, "Wouldn't it be great to be 19 and dating again?" To me the thought was absurd. I thought, "Working three jobs is superior any day of the week to being 19 and dating."

I never remembered much about dating other than getting ready and then waiting for it to be over. Dating always reminded me of gym class when it was time to be "picked" for a team. I approached the exercise with the full knowledge that I would be the last one picked. If I wasn't, I would question the intelligence and judgment of the person making the selection.

Because the origins of shame are interpersonal, it is in our most potentially intimate relationships that we feel the most threatened. We judge ourselves as we were judged by our attachment figures.

If I was asked out a second time, I either felt as though I'd fooled the individual and would prepare myself for ultimate rejection, or I'd decide that something was lacking in the person. Maybe they needed me.

I felt safest with those who needed me. It was easier to accept their desire to be in the relationship with me. I felt less threatened. When I was taking care of someone else, I didn't have to face the dependency I feared in myself.

For many, it is easier to be the one who leaves the relationship first, rather than live with the dread and anxiety of the inevitable rejection. Some people will even set up the rejection in order to feel in control of it. Many couples keep enough chaos going in the relationship that the possibilities of facing debilitating shame are reduced. It is far safer when a person feels shame about some part of themselves to hook up with an individual who is willing to act out the part of oneself that has been disowned. (This concept is explored further in Chapter Four.)

4. Adults shamed as children may appear either grandiose and self-centered (Giant) or appear selfless (Chameleon). The latter gives others the power, control and applause they deny for themselves. Both suffer enormously from internal wounds.

The face that is shown to the world by adults who were shamed as children is often the one that allowed them the greatest sense of connection with attachment figures. Wearing this "false self-disguise" offers defense and protection for the vulnerable "real self" and decreases the threat of isolation. The person who appears grandiose and power-oriented was shamed for his/her dependency and helplessness. The person who appears the most selfless and self-demeaning experienced the greatest shaming in the area of personal power. The former had to disown their shame to survive while the latter repressed their power. It is no mystery, therefore, that we are more likely to see more women that appear to be selfless and more men that appear to be grandiose, since the family and the culture have tended to shame power in women and dependency in men.

5. Adults shamed as children feel that, "No matter what I do, it won't make a difference. I am, and always will be, worthless and unlovable."

When an individual suffers from debilitating shame, it is impossible to feel lovable. Consider, for instance, the child who dawdles over her or his homework. The parent nags, the child resists. Finally the child begins the task. The parent criticizes what has been done, sighs, then does the assignment for the child. The child receives the paper back the following week marked *A* with comments from the teacher praising the child for the fine job. The praise cannot be accepted. Soon the child feels that the teacher's attention and care is only because of the *A* paper. When a person puts forth a "false self" to the world and hides the real self, there is no way to believe that acceptance is possible. It is only through disclosing our real selves that we can feel lovable. When we can voice the shameful feeling or event, the shame in that area of self is released. If I spend my life pleasing others, it is only my pleasing self that I believe can be loved. In reality, however, others in my world may love me when I disagree with them and am assertive.

6. Adults shamed as children frequently feel defensive when even minor negative feedback is given. They suffer feelings of severe humiliation if forced to look at mistakes or imperfections. To adults who experience debilitating shame, there is no such thing as a minor mistake, it's all or nothing.

Individuals who suffered consistent shaming as children may have felt a lifelong sense of inadequacy. It's not a simple matter of, "I have failed today," the internal dialogue says, "I am a failure." "My behavior isn't bad," the voice says, "I'm bad." And at other times, "You're not angry at me just this minute, you find me totally inadequate and will leave me forever as soon as you get the chance."

When we feel guilty, we feel badly for our behavior or lack of behavior — for what we did or did not do. When we feel shameful, it is our innermost being that is judged. It is not our behavior that is being judged, it is our character. The perceived attack on the self is powerful. Therefore, the defense of the self must hold equal energy. "I am not only defending me from you, I am defending me from me."

7. Adults shamed as children frequently blame others before they can be blamed.

A short time ago, I was standing in the checkout line at a department store when a couple in front of me began to fight. It didn't take long to realize that it was a disagreement where neither was interested in resolution.

"Do you have the checkbook?"

"No, why would I have it?"

"Because you had it at the grocery store last night."

"So what! It was you who wanted to go shopping today."

"Right. It's always my fault. You're always right."

"Me? Look at yourself. Was it me who forgot the grocery list, too?"

"It wasn't my list. Oh, yeah. I forgot. I'm in charge of everything."

The argument continued. Neither was willing to accept that a mistake had been made and neither was interested in finding a resolution to the problem at hand. A few minutes into the argument, the couple's daughter, who appeared to be about six years old, came from across the store to ask a question.

"Can I borrow a dollar? I forgot to get my money out of my piggy bank. I want a pink barrette to go with my new school outfit."

"Susie, you are always forgetting your money. We're just supposed to follow you around and be your maid. It's about time you learned to think for yourself!"

Now, Susie is to blame. With any luck, she can blame the dog.

What is being witnessed in this interchange is the attempted transfer of shame. Both of the adults appear to suffer from debilitating shame. Each appears to be fighting for their very lives. Each must believe the source of the problem is external in order for the self to be protected. In this family a mistake isn't a mistake. It's as if a simple matter of forgetting a checkbook becomes a hot potato that if caught, can destroy the self-concept of the person finally holding it. We become like those who search out coins on the beach with metal detectors; we are hypersensitive to the possibility of criticism from those around us. Once the threat is detected, a loud warning signal buzzes inside us and we immediately fight just to salvage our lives.

8. Adults shamed as children may suffer from debilitating guilt. These individuals apologize constantly. They assume responsibility for the behavior of those around them.

We all have had the experience of doing something against our own internalized set of values. The anxiety that accompanies transgression is guilt anxiety or fear of punishment.

For instance, if a cashier in the restaurant has given me too much change, I might instantaneously weigh the pros and cons of keeping the money. If I believe to keep it is stealing, I will let the cashier know a mistake has been made and return the money. My anxiety will be relieved when the money is returned.

Many individuals, however, live in a perpetual state of guilt anxiety. These individuals suffer debilitating guilt that is an outgrowth of debilitating shame. When a child is shamed, an immediate response to that shame is anger. Anger directed towards those we depend upon for survival, however, is often threatening to that survival. A child cannot reject the person she or he depends upon for survival. We thus feel guilty for being angry, repairing the threat of abandonment. Unlike shame, guilt is reversible. So, debilitating guilt is an attempt to repair both the interpersonal bridge and a defense against the helplessness of debilitating shame.

9. Adults shamed as children feel like outsiders. They feel a pervasive sense of loneliness throughout their lives, even when surrounded by those who love and care.

We form our identities in childhood through contact with the world around us. We believe ourselves to be that which has been reflected back to us in the eyes of those around us in childhood. When a child runs up to an adult to give them a hug and that adult turns away, looks at the child with disgust or says, "Leave me alone!", the child feels unlovable. Shame is a break in the interpersonal bond between ourselves and others. It is an intensely painful experience.

In the first chapter, for example, Perfect never felt good enough, or worthy of love. It was only through being the image that her mother needed that brief periods of acceptance were possible. She could never be perfect enough because she wasn't a giant. Loving words from her mother and others only increased her sense of shame and isolation. The feeling that, "I am not the person you think I am and who you say you care for," is one that increases internal isolation. We feel alone in our secrets and unique in our shame. "No one is as bad as I am . . . No one is as worthless . . . No one is as deformed and defective . . . Everyone else belongs somewhere. It is me alone who is unworthy of love."

10. Adults shamed as children project their beliefs about self onto others. They engage in mind-reading that is not in their favor.

I was having lunch with a friend one day when I remembered that she had recently received an award for her poetry. "Boy, you must really be excited about the award. Why didn't you call me? We could have celebrated."

"Oh. It wasn't anything," she said off-handedly. "I knew you were busy. The last thing you needed was to hear me go on and on about some silly award."

"Wait a minute," I said stunned by her response. "I would have loved to have heard about it. Come on, tell me about it."

I watched my friend become more uncomfortable. Her face turned red and she stared at the table. I knew that it was she, not me, who felt shame regarding the pride in her accomplishments. Throughout her life, her mother had accused her of being self-centered and had shamed her for bragging about her successes.

11. Adults shamed as children often feel angry and judgmental towards the qualities in others they feel ashamed of in themselves. This can lead to shaming others.

When I was a child, I remember hiding my head when the Cowardly Lion from *The Wizard of Oz* (Baum, 1936) would appear on a TV or movie screen. He disgusted me. I had a bodily reaction of malodor to him, the feeling one has when they smell something that has turned sour in the refrigerator. As a young adult I had a similar response to others who would cower or whine. Their behavior would grate on me like the sound of a nail scratching a chalkboard. It took me years to realize that I was responding to a part of myself that had been shamed and that I had disowned. I was ashamed of feeling afraid, which led me to want to control those feelings in others.

Many individuals who I have treated over the years have had a similar response to dependency in others. They got involved in relationships with dependent individuals, then sought to change them and control their dependent behavior. The term that has been given to this particular interaction is co-dependency.

12. Adults shamed as children often feel ugly, flawed and imperfect. These feelings regarding self may lead to focus on clothing and makeup in an attempt to hide flaws in personal appearance and self.

Georgia was an attractive African-American woman in her early 30s. She had referred herself for therapy because of periodic depressive episodes and lifelong low self-esteem. Additionally she was having difficulty with her finances even though she made a good salary in her position as a school administrator. She appeared for sessions dressed as if she had just stepped out of an expensive store window. Her makeup was perfect, consisting of several artistically applied layers. It looked like she was wearing a mask.

One day I commented on her appearance, "Georgia, I've seen you now for several weeks and I don't ever remember seeing you casual or relaxed. I've never seen you in casual clothes or without makeup." To this, Georgia responded in a shocked voice, "Jane, I never even walk out of the door to get my mail without my makeup."

We spent many sessions exploring Georgia's "mask." In one session, I asked her to draw a self-portrait. When we looked at it together, Georgia was surprised. She realized that she had drawn herself as a white female. "I guess I hide my 'blackness' under my expensive suits and make-up," she said with tremendous shame.

Throughout many sessions Georgia explored the shame that had developed in relation to her culture. Her family suffered tremendous cultural self-hate. And through their only daughter had attempted to erase any signs of cultural heritage.

"We were the only black family in an upper-middle-class white neighborhood. My folks would never let me play with black kids or even kids with dark skin."

As Georgia was better able to explore her early shame experiences, she appeared more relaxed in sessions. One day during her summer vacation, she appeared in my office in a slightly faded jogging outfit. She wore no make-up. "I got up late this morning. This is a come-as-you-are session. This is me without my mask! What do you think of the real me? *I* think I'm just fine, and so does my bank account." Her focus on "image" had caused her to spend thousands on makeup, hair appointments and clothes.

13. Adults shamed as children often feel controlled from the outside and from within. Normal spontaneous expression is blocked. They feel ashamed to express normal feelings such as joy, fear, anger, sexuality, playfulness or creativity. One common thought is, "I'm making a fool of myself."

Greg stood rigidly against the wall at the dance. He would seem to relax while watching others dance, but would tense up when anyone approached him. If someone came up to him, Greg would turn pink, avoid eye contact, and get nervous. At one point someone asked him to dance. He immediately responded, "No, thanks anyway, but I'm supposed to take care of the tape player." Then, Sandra yelled from across the room, "You mean you're hiding behind the tape player. Come on, dance with me. Loosen up!"

When Sandra pulled Greg onto the dance floor, he stood fixed in place, unable to move. He tried to get into the music but instead, only became more frozen and embarrassed with each beat. He later said that he thought, "Everyone was watching me make a fool of myself," when, in fact, others were enjoying themselves, unaware of his struggle.

Greg, like many adults suffering from debilitating shame, was afraid to let himself go. When children are raised in a shaming environment, they become afraid to dance to their own music. Creativity and spontaneity are exchanged for extreme overdeveloped inner controls. Many adults have never experienced sexual orgasm because they cannot allow themselves to let go internally, particularly in the presence of another.

Greg's family was critical, shaming and controlling. As a child he had felt constantly watched. "It was as if my mother and dad were just waiting for me to make a mistake. Nothing was ever good enough." In his family there was little separation between what an individual did and what they were. To make a mistake was to be a mistake. Dinner time was the worst in Greg's family. He felt grilled by his father on the day's events. "It was only safe to hold very still, eat slowly and try not to make eye contact with Dad."

Greg was now controlling himself as he was once controlled. The eyes watching him on the dance floor were first the imagined eyes of his parents, then his own. At one point he was able to joke about it, "You know, maybe I should stop taking my parents to dances."

14. Adults shamed as children feel they must do things perfectly or not at all. This internalized belief frequently leads to performance anxiety and procrastination.

For many individuals, procrastination is an attempt to defend an injured self from further shame. It is also an attempt to gain autonomy.

For instance, I may have a paper due on Thursday. If I was shamed in childhood for attempts at performance, nagged about my homework or made to feel inadequate or stupid, I won't believe I am capable of doing well on the paper. If I wait until Wednesday night to start the paper, I will have unconsciously protected myself from seeing myself as the failure I think I am.

I will also be rebelling against the voice of the nagging adult inside. I will have done it in my own time, not theirs. If I get an *A*, I will have fooled everyone or allowed myself the proud feeling of being better than those who spent all week on the paper. If I get a *C* or *D*, it is because I started the paper late. Even if I don't turn the paper in, the incomplete or *F* is in my control, not someone else's. The *F* will not carry the same feeling of shame because I was in control of it. I may feel guilty for my procrastination but I can avoid viewing myself as a failure.

Inside adults who procrastinate, there is a repetitive record set in motion every time a project is due. There is the internalized voice of a nagging significant adult figure and the voice of a stubbornly resistant, angry, guilty child who feels tremendously inadequate.

Internalized Adult Figure: "Sally, it's time to study for your mid-terms. Come on. I don't want to keep nagging you about your work this time. Just do it now. (I'll nag her until she gets it done and she'd better get a good grade for me.)"

Internalized Injured Child: "I'm going to study right away. I've got to get an *A* this time for her. (But I won't be able to get an *A*.)"

Internalized Adult Figure: "Come on, Sally. I don't want to keep nagging you. (But I will.) You want to get a good grade don't you? (You'd better get a good grade or I'll be ashamed of both of us.)"

Internalized Injured Child: "I will in just a minute. First, I'll drink some coffee. (I'll do it in my own time, not yours.) Maybe I'll clean up the house first. (I know I can do that well.)"

Internalized Adult Figure: "Sally, you always do this. You're making me angry. We've got to get that paper done. I'm not going to tell you again. (Yes I will. I know she can't do anything without me.) You want a good grade, don't you? (You'd better get an *A* or at least a *B*.)"

Internalized Injured Child: "Boy, I'm getting tired. I'll study first thing in the morning. (I'm tired of her telling me what to do. I'm angry. I wish she'd leave me alone. I'll do it in my time, not hers.) I'll get up first thing in the morning. (It won't make any difference anyway. I won't ever do as well as she wants me to do.)"

Internalized Adult Figure: "Come on, Sally. You know you won't do it in the morning. (She's going to fail, I know she is. I'm really getting anxious now. If she fails, I've failed as a parent.)"

Internalized Injured Child: "I promise I'll do it in the morning. (I feel so guilty. I've blown it anyway. I can't live up to her expectations now anyway. I've already let her down. Next time I'll start right away, then I'll do it perfectly.)"

Many parents and teachers inadvertently teach children that they are helpless failures rather than people who sometimes make mistakes. The child's work becomes the adult's work. There is no way for the child to win. There are several ways that a cycle of learned helplessness ("Nothing I do is good enough anyway"), is set in motion:

   a. By assuming responsibility for the child's work (nagging), the adult is forcing the child to become more dependent or rebel.
   b. By asking a child to do tasks they haven't learned or for which they are not developmentally capable, we set up failure. (No win.)

   c. By only focusing on one acceptable outcome (the *A*),
      an all-or-nothing thinking process is set up.
   d. By assuming too little from the child, the message
      of, "You can't do it anyway," or "What you have to
      offer isn't important," is internalized.

All of these messages become internalized as part of
the messages the adult now gives to themselves when
beginning a task.

Children, for instance, with undetected learning style
differences like dyslexia may have been considered under-
achievers in school. They may have been punished at
home and school for their lack of motivation or laziness.
The child internalizes that he will never successfully meet
the adults' expectations. He believes he is a lazy failure.

Usually this child would rather become a behavior problem or avoid school than be faced with the shame of seeing
himself as a failure. The child may experience guilt in
acting out. Guilt, however, is a far more powerful feeling
than shame because it is within his control. Helplessness
and powerlessness accompany feelings of shame. This
child, when an adult, will go through the same internal
struggle. The individual might leave a job rather than
accept a mistake or ask for help. This person may become
the company clown as a cover for feeling inadequate.

Performance anxiety could be called *shame anxiety*. If a
particular outcome on a task represents an individual's
self-worth, it will make him or her extremely anxious
about the task. In such cases, it is not performance that is
at stake, it is the self.

15. Adults shamed as children experience depression.

No one likes to be criticized or rejected. In a secure
adult, however, criticism or rejection does not mean loss
of self. But adults suffering from debilitating shame
believe that they are unworthy, defective and unlovable.
They expect to be criticized and rejected. They are
hypersensitive to any sign of judgment from others. As
children, these adults were constantly in a double bind.
They felt rejected by those they depended on for surviv-

al and self-acceptance. The normal response to criticism and rejection is anger. To be angry at the person one is dependent upon, however, is unsafe. These children, therefore, felt debilitating guilt for their anger and quickly turned anger back on themselves. In this way, they protected the relationship with the others upon whom they depended.

There are two major factors that tend to lead to depression. One is the tendency to blame oneself for the actions of others (anger turned inward), and two, experiencing a continual state of low self-esteem (to regard oneself as unlovable, unworthy, defective and dependent upon others for approval).

Brown, Harris and Bifulco published a study in 1986 on the long-term effects of loss of parental care. Lack of parental care was defined as parental indifference, neglect, overcontrol to the point of severe strictness, undercontrol wherein parents felt they were helpless in disciplining their children (children learn early that their parents can't offer the safety of external controls) and children who were sent away after sexual abuse was reported. The study showed a significant relationship between lack of parental care in childhood and depression in adulthood.

Paul had a long history of depressive episodes. His depressions seemed to be triggered by problems in his relationships with women. He had been married three times, having married his third wife 10 years ago. Paul reported feeling "hemmed in" by his wife.

"I start to feel her dependency on me and I go crazy. I just want space. I want her to stop demanding things from me. She gets angry and starts to leave. I feel confused, then angry. I don't want her to leave, I just want space. I feel relieved for a short time, but when I see her going, I panic. I feel my insides coming out. I apologize and apologize until she stays. If she leaves, even for a short period of time, I get really depressed. I don't get it. It was me asking for space, right?"

Paul was in the no-win battle he'd fought as a kid. He was terrified of his own dependency that had always felt shameful. He would get angry at his wife, as he had with his mother, for being so demanding. But as soon as she left the room, he felt guilty and apologetic, terrified to be rejected and abandoned. He depended upon his mother and then his wife for his self-esteem. He blamed himself for both the rejection (turned his anger inward), and that sense of, "My belief about myself walked out the door with her" (lack of self-esteem). The combination triggered Paul's depression.

Rejections (real or imagined) in adulthood tend to evoke debilitating shame in adults who were shamed as children. We tend to regard ourselves as we were regarded by significant adults in our childhood. We treat ourselves as we were treated. In an adult suffering from debilitating shame, even the slightest feeling of rejection will promote shame and shame triggers anger. When an individual feels dependent on the regard (or acceptance) of another for their self-esteem, anger is not safe. The feelings of anger turn swiftly into guilt, which is an attempt to repair the loss of the relationship. The anger that is not expressed is directed back on the self. The individual becomes depressed. Until debilitating shame can be healed through communication and acceptance, the cycle from shame through depression continues like a circle without end.

16. Adults shamed as children lie to themselves and others.

I was shopping in a department store with a friend one day, when I noticed a beautiful purple silk blouse on a sales rack. It had been reduced from $70.00 to $35.00. As luck would have it, it wasn't my size so I put it back. Later while in the dressing room trying on some other sale items, my friend tapped on the door. "I found the perfect blouse," she called through the door, "It's a real steal. It was $75.00 and is now only $32.00." I was astonished when she showed me the blouse later. It was the purple one I had put back on the rack.

"How much was it?" I asked, somewhat confused. "It was $32.00," she responded, "Reduced from $75.00."

When we went to lunch later that day, I peeked at the sales slip on the blouse. It was $70.00 reduced to $35.00 not $75.00 reduced to $32.00.

Why would my friend tell a lie about something so seemingly meaningless? Later I asked her. She turned bright red and looked at the floor, "I always do that. I've been doing it as long as I can remember. I don't know why. Maybe it's because I was so criticized growing up that I make it impossible for someone to criticize me now."

When children are shamed constantly for their choices, values, beliefs and actions, they learn to defend themselves by lying about seemingly trivial things. For instance, if I criticize the amount my friend paid for the blouse, or even the price it was originally, her judgment was defended because she had given me slightly different amounts. She was merely protecting herself from further wounds to her self-esteem. Unfortunately, she was still giving others the power of judgment over her choices.

17. Adults shamed as children block their feelings of shame through compulsive behaviors like workaholism, eating disorders, shopping, substance abuse, list-making or gambling.

When children grow up in an environment of shaming, they learn to believe that the solutions to problems exist only externally. For instance, Perfect could not change the fact that she was not acceptable to her mother as she was. She wasn't a giant and couldn't change that fact. She could, however, attempt to give her mother the external image that she found acceptable. Focusing on dieting and achievement was her attempt to have control and power against abandonment. It also kept the focus outside of herself, rather than feel her debilitating shame.

It was only when Perfect was seen as she really was — as a human being — and was accepted, faults and all, that she could stop focusing outside herself. Her striving for perfection as a defense against feeling her helplessness, shame, rage and potential abandonment is the dynamic many face in bulimia. The bulimic never feels good enough, pretty or handsome enough, perfect enough for the parents. They diet to be perfect, binge to get nurturing, purge anger then feel guilty.

Likewise the individual, who feels he can never achieve for himself the success or acceptability his parents or powerful others required of him, may gamble compulsively to attempt to "win the big one" and finally be powerful enough. For many compulsive spenders, having accumulated possessions is proof of their lovability or perhaps with enough layers of makeup or expensive clothing, their defects will finally be hidden. Perhaps if workaholics get that one last, "You did a good job" or applause, they can be fit to join others on the planet Earth.

Alice Miller said it well in *The Drama of the Gifted Child*, "The bigger the hole in my mother's heart, the bigger the jewels in her crown have to be." (Miller, p. 7)

When individuals lose faith in their internal resources and distrust their own acceptance, they must strive harder and harder to meet the expectations of others or find escape from the intense pain of shame. Alcohol and drugs momentarily over-ride the pain, provide the sense of power for the powerless or the loved object for the unlovable. We have all heard stories of the alcoholic hugging the bottle in an empty room. The bottle, the pills or the joint may serve as a brief substitution for a relationship with others that seems hopelessly unattainable.

Unfortunately the feelings of helplessness that accompany addiction are too familiar. The greater the addiction, the greater the power given to the addiction, and the more helpless the individual feels in breaking free of it. The individual feels helplessly dependent on the addiction for self-power or self-worth in much the same way they felt helplessly dependent on the original caretaker who found them lacking in capability, power or worth. The feelings of shame are all too familiar. Now the helplessness felt in the face of the addiction must be denied in much the same way the unacceptable qualities in the self were once disowned.

The search for external resolution — that attempt to find self-esteem, self-acceptance, control, lovability and personal power externally — only renders the self more hopeless, powerless and unworthy. And these feelings result in an increasing sense of shame and the drive to find yet another external answer.

18. Adults shamed as children often have caseloads rather than friendships.

Children who grow up in shaming environments learn early that it is not acceptable to have needs. In fact, many children are specifically shamed for needing. Statements like, "I can't believe how selfish you are," or "After all I've done for you," are typical in a shaming environment.

I once knew a child who had to kneel down before her mother's injured leg for an entire day because she, at the age of three, had screamed for her mother's help when stuck. Her mother had fallen on the stairs and blamed her child for the injury.

Adults who suffer from debilitating shame often become counter-dependent. With words and behavior, they often reflect this counter-dependency by such phrases as, "I'll do it myself, thank you," or "No one could possibly do it as well as I could." These statements accompany the feeling that having needs or needing help makes a person unworthy or unacceptable.

One defense against feeling needy is to surround oneself with others who consistently require help. Better yet, make friendships with others who have been shamed in the areas of power and independence, therefore believing they are only accepted if dependent. If one person holds needs and dependency and the other assumes responsibility and power, then neither will have to see the aspects of themselves that have previously been rejected and shamed. If I consistently take care of another, I won't have to see myself as a person that requires care. The more caretaking one does, the more dependent the other becomes. The caretaker can both assume the power in the relationship and at the same time, vicariously take care of the helpless child they once were. They may also express anger at the needs of others, thus controlling the needs they feel internally.

19. Adults shamed as children often involve themselves in compulsive processing and intellectualization as a defense against pain.

As a child I was always trying to find out the "whys" of things. At one time I searched our house in an attempt to locate the adoption papers I knew had to exist. Being adopted would provide the reasons for the pain I experienced in not feeling wanted. When I was 13, I was already intent on reading authors like Franz Kafka and Albert Camus. One of Camus' statements, "To live is to suffer, to survive is to find meaning in the suffering," was my most prized daily affirmation.

I realized much later in my life that my constant search for "whys" was my attempt to find validation for my pain and to feel connected with someone else who might have felt similarly. I also wanted to find a reason for the way I was being treated, other than the belief that I deserved it as a defective person. If I could find a reason, I could protect the image of my parents, myself and maybe even save our relationship. I was also defending myself against feeling angry at others for shaming me.

Finding validation is an important first step in the resolution of shame. It is a way of getting back some connectedness, a source of identity with others.

"Oh, that happened to you, too. I'm not alone in my shamefulness." Developing a sense of belonging in the world again is the first part in the process of resolving debilitating shame.

However, if we get stuck in the "whys," we are still accepting ourselves as helpless, hence further shame or blame, rather than as the one responsible for the resolution. When I was a young woman still stuck in debilitating shame, I would ask myself "why" when someone emotionally kicked me. I would try to convince them not to kick me again. When I was further along in the process of recovery from shame, I would search out others who may also have been emotionally kicked and could understand my experience. As an adult free from debilitating shame, I now trust myself enough to feel the pain of being emotionally kicked, tell the other to stop or remove myself from the kicker's proximity.

20. Adults shamed as children are stuck in dependency or counter-dependency.

A child who grows up in a shaming environment is not allowed his or her own autonomy. The child does not learn trust or belief in self. The child, therefore, remains dependent on the actions, words and feelings of others for approval and survival. As an adult, that child either becomes overly dependent on others or counter-dependent (a defense against feeling dependency).

Chameleon felt dependent on Giant, then Perfect, for her sense of self. Giant, on the other hand, was counter-dependent. He chose a partner who needed him. He could, therefore, feel in control of everything in his world without acknowledging his needs and dependency. As the story unfolded, however, one could clearly see that Giant was dependent on Chameleon's need to adore and be dependent upon him.

The dependent individual seems to say, "I can't do anything on my own." The counter-dependent individual seems to say, "I can do it myself, thank you," or "No one can do it as well as I can." If Perfect had not recovered from her debilitating shame, she would have had to live alone, dependent on the approval of others in her world or married a Chameleon who would need and adore her to disavow the feared feelings of dependency in herself.

21. Adults shamed as children have little sense of emotional boundaries. They feel constantly violated by others. They frequently build false boundaries like walls, rage, pleasing or isolation behaviors. If they have been physically or sexually abused as children, they will also have little sense of physical boundaries, constantly con-

fusing nurturing and sexuality, resulting in compulsive sexual interaction or no interaction.

Children who have grown up in shaming environments must constantly focus on the needs of others in order to survive. They can't develop their own needs, likes or dislikes.

As adults they cannot hold onto their own emotions when in the presence of others. If they come home and their partner is upset, they set out to take care of the other, rather than retaining the joy they felt upon coming home from work. Perhaps they receive a raise at work and wanted to celebrate. Instead they pick up the partner's feelings.

When adults shamed as children walk into a crowded room, they can identify the needs and feelings of others but have little idea of their own. If a conflict exists, it will be their responsibility to resolve it.

Children who have been sexually abused have learned there is no difference between nurturing and sexuality. They feel tremendous anxiety if not meeting the sexual needs of others. Lack of physical boundaries results in continual abuse by others or abuse of others. They might say, "I have no right to receive nurturing unless I'm sexual" . . . or, "I'll lose you if I don't have sex with you."

Lack of boundaries, both emotionally and physically, comes from constant violation of self by others. The feelings exist that I can't trust my ability to take care of myself, and I can't.

Many adults shamed as children protect themselves from loss of self in others through isolating: "I can only be a self when alone . . . Rage, come near me and I'll bite you."

Walls of distraction or dissociation are erected. "I'm watching TV . . . don't bother me . . . I'm living on the ceiling watching my life on the floor," or constant pleasing, "If I meet your needs, I can remain invisible and you can't hurt me!"

3

2-2 = 25: *The Development Of Debilitating Guilt*

A History Of Confusion

There has been a great deal of confusion throughout history, regarding the concepts of guilt and shame. Shame, for instance, was almost ignored in psychological literature until the last decade. We often talk about an individual as feeling guilty when it is actually shame that is being experienced.

"So what?" you might ask. "Is it really a big deal to confuse words?" Yes, if our confusion results in a lack of understanding of ourselves and others in ineffective therapy or in continued poor self-esteem. Our confusion of shame and guilt, furthermore, has resulted in ignoring the dynamics of debilitating guilt (being in a constant state of guilt).

For instance, I once said in a poem that adult children of alcoholics feel guilty if someone bumps into them on a crowded street (Middelton, 1980). At the time I didn't fully understand that it wasn't merely guilt that was being expressed, but instead, debilitating guilt. Debilitating guilt results from debilitating shame.

There are five major factors that have contributed to the historical confusion of guilt and shame:

1. Because of the isolating nature of shame, it is far easier to express feelings of guilt.
2. There is more personal power in the experience of guilt. We feel guilt for what we have done or not done and, therefore, have control over our future choices. When we experience shame, we feel helplessness and powerlessness.
3. When we experience guilt, we may fear punishment but when we are punished or have made amends, the guilt is resolved. When we experience shame, we

fear abandonment. There is little I can do to erase the worthless person I feel myself to be.

4. Feelings of shame and guilt frequently occur together. Helen Block Lewis (1987) states that shame and guilt are frequently fused, and, therefore, are confused. This primarily applies to debilitating guilt rather than appropriate guilt.

5. We often feel ashamed of our shame. Although we may fear punishment, there is usually relief in confessing guilt. The fear of further abandonment, however, often prevents the expression of shameful experiences or even the conscious awareness of shameful feelings.

When we experience guilt, we blame our behavior. When we experience shame, we blame our character and being. When we feel guilty, we might think, "How in the world could I have done that? How can I pay for what I've done? How can I make amends?" When we feel ashamed, we think, "What a stupid person I am. What a fool I am. Nobody likes me because I'm worthless."

Guilt is associated with wrong-doing. When we feel guilty, we feel that we owe a debt to another. Shame is associated with wrong-being or a feeling of inferiority and worthlessness. When we are shamed, there is a wound to our being and our self-esteem.

An adolescent, for example, may feel attracted to her best friend's boyfriend. She may feel guilty regarding her attraction. If, however, her friend stumbles upon the diary she has been keeping which describes her feelings for the boy, she will feel not only guilt, but also shame.

If I run into the curb while driving my friend's car, I will experience guilt for scraping the door and putting a hole in the front tire. If I have the door repaired and replace the tire, my guilt will be relieved. If, however, I grew up in a family that shamed me for mistakes, I will continue to carry feelings of shame regarding the accident. I might say to myself, "Only a fool would have done this. I wouldn't blame my friend if he never talked to me again." The expected outcome will be rejection.

What Is Appropriate Guilt?

Feelings of guilt come from our conscience, that part of us that lets us know the difference between right and wrong. Without feelings of guilt, there would be no control over our behavior. If we wanted something, for example, we'd just steal it. If we were angry at someone, we'd try to injure them physically or emotionally. Guilt comes from the limits and values our parents and other adult figures taught us which we internalized. If we have an appropriate guilt system, we learned that we should not injure another person. If we do injure another, we should atone for what we've done.

Lucy Freeman and Herbert Strean, *Guilt, Letting Go,* (1986) make clear in metaphor parts of the self previously constructed by Freud (1957). They call our unconscious (Freud's Id) the engine that powers us; the self (Freud's Ego), the driver and the conscience (Freud's Superego), our back-seat driver. It is sometimes our back-seat driver who keeps us on the road. If, however, that driver in the back seat is too harsh, it would prevent us from leaving the driveway (debilitating guilt) and if at the same time the driver was blamed for the lack of movement because of his or her worthlessness, the driver might become frozen (debilitating shame) or may avoid driving the car altogether.

In childhood an appropriate guilt system develops out of a need to be loved. I was once at a picnic with several families. Two families, in particular, caught my attention. In one family a child was being taught appropriate guilt, whereas in the other debilitating guilt and shame were in the making.

In the first family, the Smiths, Tommy, age three, and Tony, age two, were involved in healthy sibling rivalry. Tony took one of Tommy's toys and Tommy was furious. Tommy chased Tony, pulled him to the ground and was pulling on the toy, attempting to take it back. When he couldn't dislodge it from his brother's fingers, he hit him. Tony was screaming his little lungs out when June, the mother, intervened. June grabbed Tommy's little hand just before he was about to hit his brother again. "It's not okay to hit your brother!" Tommy then started screaming, "He took my toy. He's always taking my things."

"I know," his mother responded, "it's frustrating to have a little brother who is always getting into your things." June then walked over to a pile of toys, carrying Tommy with her. She picked up one of Tony's toys and brought it to him. "Tony, this is your toy. Let Tommy have his." She removed Tommy's toy and Tony started screaming. "I know it's frustrating to want your brother's toys, but it's not okay to just take them." Tony continued to scream, while June consoled them both.

After a while, Tommy said, "It's okay. Tony can have it for a little while. I'm the bigger brother. I'll share this time." June congratulated Tommy on his willingness to share and again told him that she understood his frustration. "I know it's hard to have a little brother sometimes. If you need help, let me know. It's not okay to hit, though."

Both Tommy and Tony were learning kind limits from their parent. They were learning that feelings were "okay" and understandable, but acting out those feelings in hitting and taking were not. If children can trust their parents and the loving limits they set, they will also learn to trust in themselves. They will limit themselves as the parent limited them with firmness, understanding and caring. Guilt comes from painfully learned rules, limits and values. June focused on the behavior she wanted changed, rather than her children's internal selves. As a result, Tommy and Tony will learn to set limits on themselves with kindness. They learn these limits and therefore develop a conscience because of their attachment to their mother and their need for her approval and love.

With Joey and Paul Black, however, the learning is full of anxiety, shame and debilitating guilt. Joey, age five, and

Paul, age three, were hungry. When the first hot dog was done, they both rushed toward the plate. Paul got to it only seconds after Joey. Paul grabbed it from Joey and the fight was on. Frank, their dad, who was cooking the hot dogs yelled first, "Damn it, kids, stop crying or I'll give you something to cry for." Then, Dot, their mother started yelling while still seated. "Damn it, Joey, give your brother the hot dog."

"But I got it first. It's not fair!"

"I don't care who got it first. You're the oldest."

"It's not fair." Joey yelled, still holding onto the plate.

"You're a selfish brat, Joe Black. Give your brother the food or go to the car. Why do you always have to be such a pain?"

"You can't have it. It's not fair." Joey screamed, holding the edge of the plate firmly as Paul pulled. Paul finally pulled the plate loose and the hot dog fell to the ground.

"Damn kids. Look at that, Dot. They've ruined the food. Do something with them."

At that point, Dot got up, yelling, "You're going to get it now, Joe Black. I'm tired of you. Can't even have a picnic without you ruining it. Now, get to the car. No supper for you!"

"But, it's not fair." Joey dropped the plate. "It's not fair!"

Dot grabbed Joey's arm and swatted him on the back-side, then pushed him towards the car. Joey cried all the way, saying loudly to himself, "I hate you! I hate you!"

Dot got a hot dog from Frank and gave it to Paul. An hour later, Joey was released from his car prison. He apologized to his mother, "I'm sorry I was a bad boy." His mother had saved him the hot dog that had been dropped. "Here, wash this off and eat it. I hope you've learned to stop being a selfish kid."

What were the lessons that Joey and Paul learned at the picnic?

Joey learned that his behavior was bad and so was he. He learned that he was selfish, a brat, unlovable and that he had the power to spoil a picnic. He learned that life wasn't fair, but that his feelings of frustration and anger regarding that unfairness were bad. He learned that when frustrated, you either must hit another or hit yourself (depression). He may learn to give to his brother, not out of empathy, but out of fear of abandonment. He did not learn appropriate guilt, but debilitating guilt and shame.

Both Joey and Paul learned to be ashamed of themselves for their existence. They were "damn kids" who ruined things for their adult caretakers.

Paul learned that it was all right to take things from others. He may have to keep acting up in order to get limits for his behavior. A child without external limits is a frightened child. If he can't trust his parents, he will not be able to trust himself. A child without internal limits is a child who consistently feels ashamed, afraid and internally out of control.

If this type of behavior continues, it would not be surprising to find Joe Black seeking treatment for depression in his adulthood, or find that he has been arrested for hitting his partner. He may be obsessed with fairness and feel internal rage when things aren't fair. He may experience rage if his children are served first, shame in the experience, anger at feeling the helplessness of shame. He may strike out at his children or his partner, feel guilty and then ashamed.

Or he may instead feel shame, anger, guilt and immediately turn the anger back on himself in the form of depression. Instead of developing appropriate caring, internal limits on behavior and experiencing guilt when he has violated his own value system, he may live his life suffering from the circular cycle of debilitating shame and guilt.

What Is Debilitating Guilt?

Perfect, in Chapter One, suffered from debilitating guilt. She loved her mother, and it pained her to see her mother's reaction when she would disappoint her. When upset, Chameleon would dissolve into sobs and shrink smaller and smaller. "After all," Perfect thought when her mother's demands tired her, "she has given me her whole life." Perfect even bought her mother roses on her *own* birthday to thank her for her very birth.

When we are shamed, as Perfect was, we feel inferior and helpless. We lack self-confidence, have poor self-esteem, feel self-conscious and want to hide. When we are shamed, we also feel rage. The major fear in shame is of abandonment. If we have learned, as is usual in shaming families, that to experience anger leads to abandonment, we will not feel safe in anger expression. We will either feel the anger then immediately feel guilty, and turn the anger back on ourselves experiencing depression. Or we may feel the anger, let it out, then feel guilt. Guilt, in this case, is our way of keeping the much needed adult caretaker. The experience of anger, however, is as constant as the shame, and so, therefore, is the debilitating guilt. We feel guilty if someone bumps into us on a crowded street. The more shame, the more anger, the more abandonment anxiety, the more guilt, in a never-ending cycle.

C. Peterson, S. Swartz and M. Seligman (1981) found in a sample of 87 college students, that blame of character is related to symptoms of depression. Blame of behavior, however, equated with lack of depressive symptoms. The most common dynamic in the creation of depression is the tendency to turn anger on the self and experience low self-esteem.

The Shame-Anger Cycle

Perfect could not see her mother as wrong or feel anger towards her mother and be able to survive. When she felt anger, therefore, she felt guilt immediately and turned the anger on herself. Believing that she was bad and therefore punishing herself, kept her much needed relationship with her mother intact.

A child feels helpless when shamed and gets angry at the helplessness. The child experiences anxiety for feeling anger in a shaming family because to feel anger means potential abandonment and therefore death. The anxiety leads to guilt and the anger is turned on the self, creating depression. The more shame is experienced, the more anger; the more anger is experienced, the more anxiety; the more anxiety, the more guilt; the more guilt, the more possible depression, thus we create for ourselves a vicious cycle of unhappiness and self-loathing.

Giant, Perfect's father, also felt tremendous shame and anger. He, however, let out his anger whenever he felt helpless. But the cycle continued. He expressed his anger constantly, then experienced guilt, then shame. Whether the anger felt is expressed consistently and inappropriately, or turned on the self, debilitating guilt is constant.

Suffering from debilitating guilt causes many self-defeating behaviors in adulthood. We see adults submitting to the outrageous demands of partners or employers. We see individuals who appear to be constantly angry and then almost immediately, guilty. We see adults who have felt lifelong depression. The rage felt when shamed in childhood and when suffering from debilitating shame in adulthood, is turned against the self because of the dependency on the other for survival. When we are rejected in adulthood by a mate or a lover, the feelings we experience are anger at being rejected. Furthermore, if we suffer from debilitating shame, we have not been able to gain autonomy. We continue to feel dependent upon attachment figures. It is from them, from their feelings, attitudes and opinions of us, that we feel worthwhile. To be angry at someone depended upon for felt survival causes us enormous guilt. Anger is redirected on our vulnerable self. We become trapped in a circular bind of shame, anger, anxiety, guilt and depression.

Normal Versus Debilitating Guilt

In normal guilt one feels relief from guilt when punished or when amends can be made. In debilitating guilt, however, punishment can never be attained, even through consistent self-punishment or self-deprivation. Buying her mother a present on her own birthday could not make up for the shame Perfect felt in being unlovable, the constant internal anger at feeling rejected or the guilt that accompanied the anger. The shame was constant and so was the guilt. Debilitating guilt allowed her a temporary rope swing to her mother. The emotional bridge between them, however, could not be repaired by Perfect.

Children go to any lengths to gratify their parents' spoken or unspoken needs. Children in shaming environments, however, feel trapped in double-bind requests. They are caught up in mixed messages and feel continual guilt because they must consistently fail to meet one message or the other: "Don't cry; I'll hit you until you stop . . . Be sensitive; you're a wimp if you don't fight back . . . You're lazy if you don't succeed . . . Only white kids are acceptable . . . Dress sexy and be seductive, but don't let any man touch you . . . Make up your own mind; don't argue with me . . . Be an American, but don't act like those American kids . . . Please Mother, displease Dad. Please Dad, displease Mother." Children feel angry at adults who ask them to do the impossible.

Again, anger leads to anxiety, anxiety to guilt. Anxious guilty children become anxious guilty adults.

A number of years ago, I worked with a man who suffered from debilitating guilt and chronic depression. His childhood memories included compulsively saying the rosary day and night from age 10 onward. He would say the rosary for every bad thought or deed. He went to confession daily and his constant long list of sins caused the priest to be concerned. He never felt absolved, no matter how many confessions or how many rosaries he said. When the priest tried to reassure him and tell him he needn't feel guilty for everything he felt, he began to feel suicidal, which in itself, he told me, was a mortal sin.

The young man had been raised in a Catholic family and had been shamed constantly and told he was a "bad seed." When he misbehaved, he would be strictly punished, but even after the penance, his parents would still not speak to him for weeks. He remembered a nun in Catholic school who shamed him in front of the class for lying when it had been she who had lied. As a child he felt constant shame and constant guilt. No amount of confession would relieve him of his consistent underlying anger and subsequent guilt. It was only when he could communicate his shameful feelings, fantasies and emotions that the debilitating guilt was relieved.

The Power Of Guilt

When a child is raised in a shaming environment, anger and subsequent anxiety and guilt are continuous. To a helpless child, furthermore, guilt is a far more powerful feeling than the helplessness of shame. Children can do little about the constant attacks on their characters from the outside. They can do little to feel worthy when treated as unworthy or lovable when treated as unlovable. Guilt, however, is self-directed and, therefore, a more powerful emotion. A child has a feeling of some semblance of control and power when feeling guilty.

If we imagine that debilitating shame feels inside like the equation $2-2=0$, then to feel like a zero is the ultimate in helplessness. The child, in order to add power to a powerless world, feels debilitating guilt or a state in which he or she feels power over every interaction. The equation is changed to $2-2=25$. If, as a child, I feel that I cause what is happening to me in my environment, then maybe I can change it. If I'm angry, I can apologize and make amends. At least I am in control of my feelings of anger.

If I realize I have no control over the physical and emotional violence directed towards me from my environment or if I feel total helplessness and abandonment, I won't survive. I am totally helpless. Therefore, if I am to survive, I must believe I have the power to change the external world. I cannot change my parent. In order to have a parent to nurture me, I must make them good (the fantasy parent) and myself the worthless one.

The parent of a small child can't be wrong to that child. Not to have a parent is to die.

4

Of Kings And Queens
And Haunted Castles

Erich Fromm (1956) in *The Art of Loving* said that when couples fall in love,

"... they take the intensity of the infatuation, being 'crazy' about each other, for proof of the intensity of their love, while it may only prove the degree of their preceding loneliness."

He further states,

"There is hardly any activity, any enterprise that is started with such tremendous hopes and expectations, and yet, which fails so regularly, as love." (Fromm, 1956, p. 6)

Dr. Fromm's statements may seem pessimistic. But when we examine the current divorce rate, they may seem sadly realistic.

When I was growing up, the incidence of divorce among the parents of my classmates was rare. I remember, in fact, a classmate, Susie, in fourth grade coming to school one day very sad. The teacher, when asked about Susie's sadness, told us in a whisper, "Susie feels very bad today. Her parents divorced." Although I didn't fully comprehend the meaning of that statement in fourth grade, I did know it meant at least one of Susie's parents was no longer living with her.

Today divorce is a common occurrence. To my children, it's rare to know kids whose parents have stayed together. If we look beyond divorce statistics to the number of couples who stay together and are miserable with each other, but lost without each other, Fromm's statements seem even more accurate.

At many points in my junior high school experience, I envied Susie's home situation. Her parents had not stayed together "for the children."

The Fisherman And His Wife

If we look again to fairy tales, we see many examples of kings and queens in haunted castles. "The Fisherman and His Wife" (The Brothers Grimm) is one example of a couple who seem well matched but miserable.

The fisherman, a seemingly "good-hearted man," appears incapable of standing up to his wife throughout the tale. He catches a fish who talks, who is actually a prince, and lets him go upon hearing his plea. The fisherman's wife thinks her husband foolish for letting the flounder go and even more so for not asking a reward from this talking fish. She berates his capability as a provider and demands that he ask the flounder to provide them with a cottage to replace the "hovel" the fisherman has provided. The fisherman reluctantly, and apparently unhappily, returns to the sea to request this one favor. As the story unfolds, one favor turns into many as the fisherman's wife nags and demands more. From hovel to cottage, from cottage to castle, she is still not satisfied. She wants to be King, then Emperor, then Pope — all granted but never to her satisfaction. Finally she wishes to be Ruler of the Universe. The fisherman resists asking yet another favor, then complies until the flounder can take no more of her greed and turns her great church surrounded by palaces back to the hovel from which she came.

The tale, of course, is one that focuses on the liabilities of greed, but what of the relationship between the fisherman and his wife? It certainly isn't a marriage "made in heaven," or is it? Why is it so difficult for the fisherman to stand up to his wife and act on his own behalf? On the other hand, why is it that she can never get enough to satisfy her longings? Why would she commit to a partner for whom she apparently has so little respect? Why would he marry an individual who respected him so little? What was the original attraction, and what held their marriage together?

Cinderella

What of the prince in Cinderella? He proclaims that he will marry any woman whose foot fits the slipper. On Cinderella's part, however, we can clearly see that riding away with any prince who appears half decent, is certainly better than her home situation. Yet even this is suspect. There is no courtship, no getting to know each other, just "happily ever after." One might question, furthermore, why any father who apparently loves his daughter, as the story purports, would allow such treatment of his child by his mate. There is very little mention of his relationship with the wicked stepmother. It is highly unlikely, however, that they have much communication. Furthermore, it's amazing that so many children are given away in fairy tales for the misdeeds, desires or past lives of their parents, or is it?

If we search our memory, most of us can recall at least one acquaintance or relationship that reminds us of Cinderella's relationship with the prince, her parents' relationship or that of the fisherman and his wife. Their partnerships certainly weren't made in heaven. Their coupleships were instead the result of shame-based childhoods.

A part of each partner's self was sacrificed for their survival in a shaming family or community. Sadly the adults who shamed these children were themselves products of shaming environments. Like magnetic forces, these adult children are drawn to those who possess their disowned parts. They are equally repellent to individuals who do not possess, or are unwilling to act out, the parts of themselves they desperately want back, yet at the same time, need to control.

The fisherman appeared to be a selfless man, while his wife held his desires for unmet needs. She, on the other hand, gave him the dependency she was terrified of in herself. His wife held his unconscious anger and hostility, while he held her powerlessness and overt feelings of shame. As long as the fisherman's wife was willing to act out her mate's anger, he could experience himself as completely without anger. He could enjoy the products of her greed while remaining selfless. She could deny her dependency needs, while he acted them out for her. It is not difficult to imagine the adult world from which each sprang.

In partnerships we tend to fight in each other the very thing that attracted us with such force. We are attracted by the emotion, the trait, the characteristic that we then seek to control. We will even see an emotion, such as anger, in a partner that isn't there, if normal expression of anger was shamed in us as children. We will then seek to control the anger in the other as we have in ourselves for a lifetime. The cycle repeats itself in an endless repetition of blaming, controlling and defending. The argument frequently ends with one partner's guilty apology, rendered out of an anxious childhood need for survival, rather than sincere communication. Sometimes the interaction doesn't end. Stubbornly held walls finally crumble and the conflict is swept under the rug until the next time. It appears as if each partner is fighting for their lives because inside they are.

Projective Identification

Melanie Klein (1955) first labeled the interaction in which one individual projects onto another a disowned part of themselves as *projective identification*. In *projective identification* one person induces another to act in a particular way. It was through Klein's early work that a number of questions regarding interactions in families were answered.

Understanding projective identification allows us to understand why a child who has been sexually abused (therefore having tremendous shame regarding their sexual self) might marry a partner who is sexually demanding. They may be originally attracted to the partner's sexual spontaneity, which has been so abused and shamed in themselves. After a commitment is made, however, the attraction disappears and they may reject the partner's advances or condemn themselves to repetitive sexual interactions where only their partner receives sexual satisfaction. A child with a depressive parent, may couple with an individual who is depressed, thus relieving their own terror of depression. Therefore, our intimate partner often becomes the mirror reflection of the part of ourselves that has been shamed and disowned so long ago.

When we understand the ramifications of shaming childhoods, we begin to understand why we become almost addictively attracted to individuals who our closest friends may have told us are not good for us. If we can understand the workings of lifelong shame in our relationships, it will help us to see why the home we so happily built with Prince Charming or Florence Nightingale, has become a haunted castle. We will be more understanding of our willingness to remain in abusive relationships for which we feel tremendous shame. The abusive husband may deny his own dependency, but behave in such a way in relation to his wife, she assumes a dependent position. He does not have to be conscious of his own dependency needs and she does not have to be conscious of her need to abuse others. The complementary abusive and dependent positions of each create a balance of the marital system (Crisp, 1988).

When we understand the workings of debilitating shame and guilt in partner selection, it becomes clear that Perfect, in Chapter One, would most likely choose a chameleon for her mate. Although she may wish for a giant and shame herself for not being worthy of one, she will feel most comfortable with a chameleon who will hold her dependency as her mother once did. She can with a chameleon for a partner continue to be the perfectionistic workaholic who focuses on the needs and demands of another, rather than face the pain of her own unmet needs. She will avoid facing the pain of a lost childhood. However, at the same time, she will attempt to resolve her painful past by living it a thousand times over. She may become angry at her mate's dependency, shaming him for his needs, as she shames herself, while unconsciously sabotaging any attempts of the partner to become autonomous. If she faces her shame and the pain of past losses, learns to trust herself and another and takes back her once disowned parts, her attractions to others will change. She then will only be comfortable choosing a partner who is a whole human being like herself.

Giant could not accept his imperfections, dependency, fears or shame. Chameleon could not face her strength, power or anger. They matched. Together they made a whole. As alluded to in the fairy tale, Giant was reared by a chameleon who needed him to be tough and powerful, while Chameleon's mother was a giant who required her dependency, adoration and powerlessness. Our legacies of shame pass down generationally like the family jewels, linens and photograph albums. In our partners and children, we look for that which was shamed and disowned in ourselves. When we are nurtured and allowed to become autonomous human beings, we seek intimacy, communication and companionship with our partners. When we are shamed, we seek survival. It is far more difficult to leave a partnership of desperation than one of choice.

How Can We Tell If Our Castles Are Haunted?

Over the last number of years, the question I am asked most consistently by individuals who have been involved in repetitive dysfunctional relationships is, "How will I know if I've become involved in another relationship that is not in my best interest?" It is important to understand that we become involved in relationships that are not good for us out of survival. On one level we have learned from our primary caretakers that, "This is the way to form a relationship. This is love." On another level, this is the way we've learned how to survive. Deep down, we have a great deal of anger at "being forced to disown a part of ourselves in order to have a relationship with the other."

It is important to allow ourselves to feel the pain of living in haunted castles. It is only through facing the shame that the generational cycle of shame can end. It is also important not to re-shame ourselves in the process.

When an individual grows up in another country, he or she learns the customs, language, gestures and cultural expectations of that country. If the person moves to another country, he or she will try to find those in the new area who speak their language and understand their customs. In a similar way, we learn how to form relationships from our earliest primary caretakers. We learn the language, customs, gestures, values and expectations of our family culture. We seek to find a partner with similar and complementary expectations. As painful as it may be, sometimes this is what we've learned in order to love and be loved. In the following part of this chapter I will explore several characteristics of the impact of childhood debilitating shame in adult relationships.

1. We lose ourselves in love.

Many years ago, while waiting for a table in a restaurant, I ran into a friend I had not seen for a long time. I had written her often, but she had not responded to my letters since her marriage ten years before. We introduced each other to our partners and the four of us decided to have dinner together.

I was astonished by my friend's behavior. It was as though she had become another person. She was quieter and more anxious where before she had been outgoing. She was no longer pursuing the interests that before had been extremely important to her. She had lost track of all the friends she had prior to her marriage, and it appeared from the conversation that she hadn't made new friends. When I would ask questions about her current life, her partner would answer for her or interrupt her answer. It was as though Joanne had lost the core of herself.

When we went to the ladies room together later on in the evening, I was shocked to see a totally different person emerge. She was my old friend again. She laughed and joked. She told me how much she had wanted to see me and other old friends. She told me that she missed her art and music terribly.

When I asked her why she had given up so many parts of her life, she replied, "Sid needs to be the center of my world. He was very jealous of the time I spent on my art and music. He never wanted to meet my old friends.

"I get very lonely and depressed sometimes. Well, you understand, you have to make sacrifices. Sid says he wants me to have my own interests but he shows me in a million ways that he doesn't.

"When we were first engaged, I had just been juried into my first art show. I was so excited and proud. Sid was supposed to pick me up at my house so we could have our own celebration dinner. He was going to escort me to the opening. But he didn't show up. I called and called. He finally got to my house an hour after the opening started. Would you believe it, I missed my own opening. Well, you know I couldn't leave without him. What if he'd been in trouble or hurt? He apologized and told me that he'd got tied up with a female colleague at work who desperately needed to talk with him about a problem in her personal life.

"It didn't take too many incidents like that to finally get the message. Sid's mother had spent all of her time working. I realized that he just couldn't stand to compete with my interests as he had with hers. Those are just sacrifices we have to make in a marriage, right?"

Later that evening, I realized that Joanne's family had also been full of mixed messages. She was told that her parents were proud of her talents, but they never came to her special events. She had never introduced me to her family. She had told me that it made her mother too nervous to have kids around. Her parents never visited her in college. She went home often to help her mother out with one thing or another. Joanne had spent a lifetime rationalizing painful losses.

2. When we argue, we fight for our lives.

When couples who were once shamed as children conflict, they fight as if their entire being depended on winning. Their arguments have winners or losers and are centered on right or wrong. The emotions in each partner are often far greater than the issues of the conflict warrant. I've known couples to stop speaking for days over who fed the dogs or the right and wrong way to squeeze a tube of toothpaste. There appears to be little interest in resolving the issues being discussed. Instead, there appears to be an issue under the issue that is not being verbalized, "I need you to share my view so that I'm not wrong. I need you to validate my reality. I need to be right so that I'm not wrong. I can't have an opinion or perception unless you agree with me."

The same conflicts seem to recycle again and again, each time with more emotional energy than the last. It appears as though partners are saving issues like one would collect green stamps. "You still haven't apologized for what you did to me 15 years ago. I'm still angry. You'll never to able to make up to me for the time you . . ." When a partner collects enough books of stamps, the collection can be turned in for a guilt-free divorce, an affair or simply the right to get back at the other in order to even the score. The books of stamps serve as protection against further wounds to a vulnerable self.

I often tell couples that when the emotions in an argument are more than the situation warrants, they are living in another time zone. Instead of resolving the issues at hand, they are unconsciously expecting the other to heal the injuries of the past.

As Harriet Lerner said so well in *The Dance Of Intimacy* (1989),

> "We become like the proverbial man who had too much to drink and lost his keys in the alley but looked for them under the lamp post because the light was better."

Our partner agreeing to squeeze the toothpaste in a particular way is not going to erase the childhood pain of being constantly shamed for the way he did things. We cannot regain ourselves from another. Having our reality validated in an argument does not change the belief that we need another to validate what we feel, think or believe.

The "I'm sorry," or "You're right," fought for with such force, doesn't heal the wounds of a shamed past. The words seem in the end sadly empty. We don't know why. We fight for more validation, more power from our partners. We don't believe the words when we hear them. The cycle continues.

3. We expend a great deal of energy in mind-reading. We frequently talk to ourselves more than to our partners.

When we grow up in a shaming environment, we learn early to protect ourselves from more pain. We often become hypersensitive to the needs and demands of others in an attempt to remain invisible. We attempt to minimize the wounds to our already injured ego. It was important in childhood to guess at the other's needs and wishes and attempt to fulfill them in order to fight off more injury. We carry this attempt at invisibility into new relationships, expecting our partners to judge us like our adult caretakers once did if we allow ourselves to be vulnerable.

Jerry: "I thought you were going to take that course at the community college."

Suzanne: "No, I decided not to."

Jerry: "Why? I thought you were looking forward to the course."

Suzanne: "I knew you really didn't want me to take it."

Jerry: "But I told you I was willing to watch the kids on Tuesday night. I told you I wanted to support you taking the class."

Suzanne: "I know. That was nice, but I know you didn't really mean it. It was nice of you to say so anyway."

Jerry: "But I did mean it!"

Suzanne: "It's all right. I don't mind."

Jerry became an actor in Suzanne's play of the past. No matter what he says, she believes that he doesn't really support her wishes and needs. Suzanne was raised in a family where her needs were shamed. She was constantly considered selfish by her parents.

Linda: "Why didn't you tell Teresa that you wanted friends over this weekend?"
Joyce: "Because she doesn't like to have my friends over."
Linda: "I thought she liked your friends."
Joyce: "Well, not really."
Linda: "Did she tell you not to have them over?"
Joyce: "Well, not exactly, but I know how she feels."
Linda: "Joyce, did you talk to Teresa about it?"
Joyce: "No, I didn't have to. I just knew."

Joyce has had a conversation with Teresa in her mind. She asked the questions and answered them herself as she had learned to do with her parents. Joyce was shamed by her mother for asking questions. Her mother's favorite sentence was, "Joyce, I can't believe you are asking me. You know I don't like . . . You're just trying to irritate me."

Sometimes the answers we give ourselves when we read our partner's mind enrage us, even though our partner has never had the opportunity to be part of the conversation.

Ted: "I wish just once you'd value my opinions. I'm tired of you treating me like a stupid idiot. I'm not, you know."
Kay: "I don't think you are stupid. I do value your opinions. What are you talking about?"
Ted: "Right! Look, I know what you think of me!"
Kay: "What are you talking about? When didn't I listen to an opinion of yours? I feel supportive of your choices."
Ted: "Sure! Let's just drop it. I know what you think of me."

Ted feels shamed by Kay regarding his opinions when, in fact, he rarely offers an opinion. He feels shamed by her, then furious at being shamed. He doesn't need Kay to be part of the conversations. He asks the questions and answers them himself. The ghosts of his past are constantly part of their communication.

4. We pay a high price for those few good times.

Growing up in a shaming environment is enormously painful. Many of the individuals I know have shared diaries with me that they kept when they were children. It is obvious that they have clung to those few good times.

Clinging to happy times allowed us to believe we were safe, secure and loved. It allowed us to protect the relationships we had with adult caretakers. It allows us to nurture ourselves. We learned that bad times are just the expected price we paid for moments of happiness. We expect the same from adult relationships. When we feel disappointed in our adult partners, we immediately remember that week two years ago when everything was wonderful. We feel ashamed of our selfishness. We might say to ourselves, "What's the matter with you? You're never satisfied."

Tammy began seeing me in counseling after seven years of marriage. She felt miserable much of the time. Like many adults who were shamed as children, she originally wanted therapy to enable her to cope better with a miserable marriage. She wanted to change herself so she could be more "lovable."

Her husband was rarely at home. He would stay at the office until all hours, never calling to say he was going to be late. When he did come home, she would feel he'd been with someone else. He took little interest in Tammy or their children. He did nothing towards the upkeep of their home. He often said that he just needed his freedom. Tammy would be shamed when she questioned him about his lateness or about forgetting their son's birthday. He said she was a nag who was never satisfied. Throughout her childhood, her father had also told her she was never satisfied when she asked for anything. She felt great shame at wanting more.

When she first started seeing me, she would balance everything. "I felt really angry when Paul forgot Tommy's birthday but he's really a good father. He took Tommy to the movies a couple of months ago. Sometimes it feels like

I'm married, but I don't really have a husband. It's like he's away in the military or something. I shouldn't complain though. He took us on a wonderful trip last year. It was a lot of fun. He really loves us, I know he does. He tries hard. He just needs his freedom."

5. We often sign two contracts upon commitment, one conscious and another that's unconscious.

Most of us remember our wedding vows or the promises we made when we made a commitment to our partners. Few of us were aware, however, that we made another unconscious commitment early in our relationships. Our unconscious commitments are often based on the defenses we've developed in shaming families.

Some examples of unconscious contracts are:

a. I'll be the sick one. You can be the healthy one. You can take care of me and feel good about yourself. I can feel bad about myself and be irresponsible.

b. I'll promise to keep distance and appear to be rejecting. You can be the pursuer and feel rejected. Together we will keep the comfortable distance we each need.

c. I'll disappoint you and you can punish me.

d. I'll get my needs met and feel guilty. You can get none of your needs met and feel victimized and superior.

e. I'll keep distracted if you will.

f. I'll keep up a wall and feel protected. You can try to break through it and believe you are capable of intimacy.

g. I'll play your mom if you'll play mine.

h. I'll play your dad if you'll play mine.

i. I'll play your mom if you'll play my dad.

j. I'll play your dad if you play my mom.

Because of the overwhelming pain experienced in our first relationships, true intimacy with our adult partners is often frightening. Unconscious agreements are established to pace the distance and closeness in relationships. They also provide us with the opportunities to work through the emotions resulting from the debilitating shame of a painful past. There are as many "contracts" as there are couples. You might wish to explore the possible unconscious agreements in your relationships.

6. We blame and are blamed.

Children who grow up in shaming environments quickly learn that one must blame or be blamed. There are very few compromises in shaming environments. It often feels like we are playing "emotional hot potato" in our adult relationships. Either our partner is wrong, or we must be. As explained earlier, when we grow up with debilitating shame, we don't make mistakes, we are mistakes. Passing the blame to someone else is our attempt to protect an already injured self from more wounds.

7. We want them gone, then fight to get them back.

Grace and Tom had been separated six times in their ten-year marriage. The pattern was always the same. After a period of separation, Tom would pursue Grace. They'd begin dating, then "fall in love" again. They would eventually reunite without really talking about what the separation had been about. They would be blissfully happy for about a year, then Tom would start finding fault with Grace's behavior. She was too smothering. She was too distant. He would tell her that she needed counseling. She would become angry. He would feel victimized by her anger. After a time, he would say he was no longer in love with her and wanted her to move out. She would try to persuade him to get into marital counseling.

"It's not me with the problem," he would say. "All I want is a partner who is capable of being intimate. It's you with the problem." They would finally separate. Grace would get an apartment. Tom would remain in the house. Grace would begin to rebuild her life. After some time had passed, Tom would feel "lost without her" and want her to come home.

Like Perfect in Chapter One, Tom had grown up in a shame-based family. Tom's mom had been an alcoholic who showed she needed her son to be 50 at five, yet shamed him constantly. The shame was always shown in either silent rejection, which usually would occur when Tom showed independence or stated an opinion that differed from his mother's. Sometimes Tom would be openly shamed when his mother was drunk. Her favorite words to Tom were, "Who do you think you are anyway?" Tom, like Perfect, attempted to fill all of his mother's wishes for her.

When he was a child, he felt that if he did everything perfectly, his mom would be happy and stop drinking. Sometimes Tom would have glimmers of hope. Tom and his mother, for instance, were very close when they were on vacations as at these times, his mother would not drink. His father was a seaman who was only home every six months. Tom's mother wouldn't drink as much when his father was around.

With Grace, Tom was acting out the patterns and emotions of a painful past. He had one foot planted on the doorstep, ready to run. He both craved and feared dependency. Furthermore, with Grace, he was able to act out both the intense feelings of longing to be accepted by his mom, while also expressing the shame-based anger he could not express throughout his childhood. It was only when he knew he could have Grace's unconditional loyalty that he could experience the anger of an old shame-based attachment.

For Grace's part, she said she felt like a yo-yo.

"First he wants me, then he doesn't. One day I'm going to walk out and never come back."

Grace had grown up in a family that ran both hot and cold. Sometimes the parents would totally focus on the children. At other times, they would give Grace the feeling they wished she'd disappear. Their inconsistency related to the degree of their interests in their work, hobbies and the world outside the home. In other words, the kids were there for them when they needed them.

8. We know it will be different but expect it to be the same.

Over the years, through my own experiences and listening to the experiences of others, I have realized that when we grow up in families of shame, we expect what we get in relationships. "But I don't," you may protest. I believe we know our partner and what to expect in the relationship very soon after our first meeting. We then set out to convince ourselves that we know something different. After all, would we really feel good about making a commitment to someone who always has let us down, criticized us, shamed us, never shown up on time or treated us as invisible? Soon after the commitment is made, we begin to sense that this commitment isn't the answer to our prayers. We may, in fact, feel as badly about ourselves in the relationship as we did in our shaming families and communities. We ignore that information, however, and say we expect something different from the relationship.

I knew a couple in college who had been going together since high school. They complained about each other constantly. One would tell me, "I wish just once that she'd do what she tells me she will." The other would say, "I wish just once he'd let me live my own life. I feel smothered by him."

One day I asked them both what they expected from one another in the relationship. The first friend told me that he expected her to be sincere, consistent, loving, nurturing and honest.

"I thought you said you could never trust what she told you, that she was always late for dates and sometimes wouldn't even show up."

"Well, that's true, but that's not what I expect."

Then I asked the partner, "What do you expect from him in the relationship?"

"Well, I expect him to respect me and my way of doing things. I expect him to love me for myself and let me be myself."

"But, I thought you felt smothered by him and criticized," I stated.

"Yes, but that's not what I really expect."

My friends married and are still fighting over expectations. They also say, "I wished I'd known that before we got married." The fact is, they did. They expected what they knew to be untrue about each other, then spent years fighting about those expectations. They felt let down and devalued just as they had in their childhood.

9. We often feel that our partners are controlling our behavior.

Adults who grew up in shaming environments often feel controlled in relationships. It is true that there is a sense of being a puppet or reverse-puppet in relation to our partners. The control we exert on ourselves, however, is from within us, not outside of us. We often find partners who look to us for the disowned parts of themselves. These individuals may seek to control that disowned behavior in us. It is us, however, who exerts the control internally.

We learned throughout our childhood that the only way to have a relationship with another was to give up large parts of ourselves. If Perfect, for instance, coupled with a chameleon, she would feel that her partner was making her take care of her or him. She might feel that she had to lift their depression, take responsibility for their moods, wait for them even if it made her late and, generally, make sure things were perfect. Soon she might resent her life of being super woman who had to change her clothes in telephone booths. She may not realize that the demands are coming far more forcefully from the inside than from without. The self-expectations formed were real ones. Her mother had expected her to be more than herself from birth. It was the expectations from that first primary relationship pulling the strings inside her, not her adult partner. The belief that we must fulfill another's needs or, in some cases, resist and do the opposite of what is requested, comes from the terror of the abandonment of self in childhood. A child can be emotionally and physically abandoned by a parent or adult caretaker. An adult may be left but not abandoned by a partner. It is the fear of abandonment in childhood, not adulthood, that brings the ghosts to our new castles.

10. We are frequently attracted to the emotional qualities in another that we have disowned in ourselves. The characteristics in the other that attracted us with such force is often the part of the other that angers us later in the relationship. We often attempt to control in the other, the part of us that was shamed in childhood.

A child who was shamed for their dependency in childhood, may select a partner who is overly dependent. The adult child might then attempt to control the dependency in the other. This interaction is sometimes referred to as co-dependency. A child, who was shamed for their anger, might choose an abusive partner. Likewise, the partner might have been shamed for their helplessness and choose a partner who acts out the helplessness. Each will try to control in the other that which has been disowned in themselves.

11. We often create triangles in relationships.

Relationship triangles and looped communication are characteristic of shame-based families. For instance, in order to talk to Dad, we might have been required to talk through Mother. When a parent is angry at the other parent, they might have talked to their child about their unhappiness. Dad might be angry at his own mother, yet, it is his partner who acted out the anger.

Relationship triangles help us to pace closeness and distance in our intimate relationships. Having someone in the middle offers protection against both intimacy and abandonment. It keeps the relationship distant and safe while at the same time, providing the glue for the relationship. Looped communication and relationship triangles allow the focus to be redirected away from the vulnerable self.

A couple, for instance, might rarely be alone. They may have had one person or another staying with them throughout their married life. They may first focus together on helping out a friend who needs a place to stay and later unite over the problems they are having with the friend.

There are often as many triangles as there are couples. Some of the triangles that we are most familiar with may be: affair triangles, heat off the marriage onto the children triangles, let you and her or him fight triangles, victim . . . persecutor . . . rescuer triangles, incest triangles and in-law triangles.

When we attempt to withdraw from triangular looped communication in our families, we might constantly feel like a traffic cop.

"Mother, you'll have to talk to Dad if you're angry at him."

"Sam, you need to straighten that out with your mother. I'm not her."

Sometimes when we stop participating in these communication loops and hold others responsible for their communication, we see for the first time the extent to which we have been living in triangles.

12. We seek the unconditional love from our partners that we didn't adequately receive in a shaming childhood.

One of my favorite statements in relationships prior to my recovery from debilitating shame was, "You should have known." This statement applied to many things that I wanted from another but never requested. I expected others to read my mind and to know my needs without stating them. When I wanted help with something or needed a hug, I expected the other to fulfill my needs without asking. I would resent the other for not giving me something that I had never asked for. I used to think, "If I have to ask, then it's not worth it."

There is a time in all of our lives when we were entitled to get our needs met without asking. That time has long since passed now that we are adults. As little children we were entitled to adult caretakers who would know what we needed. We were entitled to be fed when hungry, to be nurtured and held when upset and to be sought out and comforted when we looked disappointed. We were entitled to a time in our life when we could express anger without the other becoming defensive at our outbursts.

I once heard a woman friend of mine who was in the process of learning to state her anger, yell at her partner, then, when her partner defended himself, she stated, "I can't believe you're upset with me. I'm learning to state my anger directly. I thought you would be pleased." It seems odd to expect an adult partner to be joyful and relieved that we're getting our anger out by yelling at them. This expectation is from our child self, not the adult we have become.

Unfortunately, as adults, we need to ask for what we need. We are no longer entitled to have someone read our minds. We pay the consequences for our adult anger. Our partners will hold us accountable for our emotional outbursts when practicing new emotions. It is very painful to realize that we will never be five years old again. That time has long since passed. We are no longer entitled to unconditional love. It is not our partner's responsibility to read our minds or to meet our needs without us stating them directly.

5

Goldilocks And The Three Bears

The Search For Just Right

In the folk tale, *Goldilocks and the Three Bears,* Goldilocks set out for a walk in the woods one day and discovered a cottage owned by a family of three bears. The bears were not at home so Goldilocks entered. She was enticed, it would seem, by the aroma of porridge wafting from bowls on the table. Being very hungry, she decided to help herself. First she tried the largest bowl of porridge. It was much too hot. The next size bowl of porridge was definitely too cold. But the contents of the smallest bowl was just right so she ate it all up.

After such a good meal, Goldilocks felt tired so she went to the bedroom. The first and largest bed was much too hard for her. The middle-size bed was way too soft. But the smallest bed was just right and she fell fast asleep. Well, as luck would have it, when Goldilocks had just fallen asleep, the family of three bears returned from their walk and discovered her. She was so frightened when she saw them looking at her that she ran out of the house and all the way home. Furthermore, she decided never to enter those woods again.

Like Goldilocks, many adults who were shamed as children have spent a lifetime searching for "just right." Many have come from "too hot" families and others from "too cold." Many adults who were shamed as children had adult caretakers who were "too hard" and too strict, while others had their world full of adults who were "too soft" and couldn't set limits and follow through.

Goldilocks and the Three Bears lacks many of the features of a true fairy tale. There is little consolation for poor Goldilocks. The tale neither has a happy ending or any resolution of conflict. Similarly, many adults shamed as children promise themselves that they will create a "just right" family in their adulthood. Without recovery from the effects of debilitating shame, however, "just right" is rarely created. Many times "happily ever after" is not within reach. It is also difficult to attain resolution of the conflicts with the families who once shamed us. Members of "too hot" and "too cold" families are often in so much pain and denial that an adult-child member of the family who seeks resolution from past conflicts is rarely heard. In fact, they are continually shamed even more.

"Too Hot" Families

One type of "too hot" family is the family in constant crisis. In this family, there is little consistency from one hour to the next. Rules are inconsistent, emotions are expressed in an unpredictable manner and boundaries are constantly violated in one way or another. The consistent intrusions contribute to the child's sense of powerlessness and helplessness. In these families shaming is overt. There is frequent parental neglect and physical, emotional or sexual abuse.

The children in these families may express feelings of not being wanted, being in the way or the cause of the family's problems. Love and affection are rarely expressed and when spoken, they are conditional. Anger is often pervasive, explosive and unpredictable. Feelings related to shaming and violence are stifled. Children learn to turn the anger back on themselves and become 50 at five or model themselves after other members of the family and suppress the anger, then explode. Other children seem forgotten altogether and spend their lives roaming the neighborhood looking to strangers to meet their needs. All children in the family suffer from debilitating shame and guilt. "Families in perpetual crisis appear to be dancing around a pit of emptiness. One false move and they can fall." (Kagan and Schlosberg, 1989, p. 5)

The family messages in the chaotic "too hot" family seem to be: "Don't ask questions. Don't trust anyone.

Every person for themselves. You're too much for us. I hit you because I love you. You're asking for it if you upset us. Don't do as I say, do as I do!"

A few months ago I had the rare experience of actually having almost three hours between flights at O'Hare Airport in Chicago, usually I'm running to catch a connecting flight. I was moving from one gate to another through the underground tunnel in the United terminal. I was taking my time, looking at the beautiful lighting display on the ceiling as I stood on the moving sidewalk. Just ahead of me I saw a mother and her child. The child was looking at the lights, too, as they changed from one beautiful color to another. Her mother was pulling her along by her little arm and yelling at her at the same time.

"Damn it, hurry up. What's the matter with you. I suppose you want me to carry you. Well, you've got another thought coming, you little brat!"

Finally, the mother tugged so hard that she pulled the little girl face down on the sidewalk.

"Damn it! Get up! You really are a pain!"

She then pulled the child's little arm straight up, yanking her to her feet. She held her in the air by the arm as the child screamed. I moved up to the pair and asked the mother if I could be of some assistance. (A number of years ago I decided that I would no longer watch abuse without attempting to intervene.)

"Yes, you can carry her!" the mother snapped.

I picked up the child and she immediately cuddled against my chest, whimpering, "My arm hurts; my arm hurts." I realized by the child's immediate trust of a stranger that this behavior had happened before. She had few boundaries for a three-year-old child. I comforted her and talked to her about the beautiful lights all the way to the gate. I was surprised when I got to the gate that it was my plane the two were also taking. With over two hours before departure, I wondered what the rush was. I soon found out.

"Will you watch her for a few minutes?" the mother said nervously.

"Sure," I responded. "But I don't know if she'll feel comfortable with a stranger."

"Yeah, she will. She's not usually a pain like she was down there."

"She wasn't a pain," I responded. "She's just a bright curious little girl."

"Yeah, well, whatever," the mother said nervously, and then ran off.

I waited for the mother's return for an hour. The little girl, Susie, didn't seem to be concerned about her mother's disappearance. She just talked with me as if trying to entertain me. She acted in many ways like a little adult. When her mother returned, the parent reeked of alcohol. Now I knew what the hurry was. The mother was at that stage of intoxication where she talked nonstop. "Thanks for watching her. God, I hate these trips. I'm visiting my mother and I hate it. I can never do anything to please her."

"Like you seem to feel about your daughter sometimes?" I responded.

"Well, I guess," she said, surprised by my straightforwardness. "But, not really. My mother's a chronic alcoholic."

Susie's mother was projecting onto Susie many of the feelings she felt about herself. She was playing hot potato with shame. Unfortunately, Susie's got the potato. Before the age of five, this child is learning that she's in the way, is unwanted, unlovable and "a brat." The good news is that even in the mother's intoxication, she was able to hear my words to her that day in our conversation before the flight. I received a note later that she had entered an alcohol treatment center. The bad news may be that the alcoholism may be treated and the generational shame may remain invisible.

Too Hot: Chaotic

In chaotic "too hot" families the pain of the past is carried into the present. Legacies of alcoholism, physical, emotional and sexual abuse travel down generational lines. They may be families of depression, war survivors, religious fanaticism, constant moving or frustration built on generational shame of poverty and cultural self-hate. The children in these families suffer from direct verbal and physical shaming and also the shame of feeling ashamed of their parents. They may feel different in school compared to other kids and may wear masks of shame in the world as well as at home.

Two other types of "too hot" families are the overprotective enmeshed family and the victim family. Children in both families suffer from both overt and covert shaming but there is less physical violence than the prior example. In the overprotective family the strictness is often more consistent than the first example, but there is so much that a child can't do. There is little you can do, in fact, without experiencing shame and guilt.

Too Hot: Overprotective

The message, "I'm doing it for your own good," is paramount in the overprotective family. The extreme rules, however, stem from the parent's traumatic and shameful past. The adults rigidly protect the children from their own unresolved pain and debilitating shame experiences. In the overprotective "too hot" family the world is seen as a hostile, dangerous and often sinful place. The child is bound by invisible ropes to the parent. The child sets off to take her first steps away and runs into the parent's barricade of, "Don't," or, "You'll hurt yourself." The child becomes ashamed of her own independent desires and terrified of the world. Decisions are constantly being made for the child. Sometimes homework is done for her. The child is usually not allowed to contribute to their world because adults can do it better. As is obvious, there are constant violations of emotional boundaries. Parents frequently listen in on phone calls, open mail and search rooms for evidence of possible danger. The child's friends are constantly suspect, "He/she only wants you for your"

. . . The child grows up to feel both terrified and personally incompetent. The shame is enormous, so is the debilitating guilt because after all, "Everything was done for the good of the child."

Adult members of "too hot" overprotective families often have enormous unresolved grief throughout their lives. Maybe there was a child who died before who was never grieved. Sometimes the parents were victimized in their own childhoods through war, physical abuse, sexual abuse, rape or unresolved family deaths.

Timmy was afraid to come to school. His mother would always bring him, complete with long lists of instructions for the teacher. She would look worried when she left and would tell him, "Please be careful." Timmy was obviously terrified. He'd cry when she left and then seem frozen. Furthermore Timmy always seemed to have one illness or another and was constantly being taken to the doctor. He was afraid to explore and try new things. He seemed afraid to attempt anything on his own and constantly feared making mistakes, whether in the classroom or outside at recess. He was frightened and ashamed constantly. After a while, the other kids began taunting him, "Timmy's a mommy's boy. What's the matter Timmy, are you a scaredy cat?"

Timmy's mother had suffered the death of a child before Timmy was born. The death of the child was never grieved. His mother felt tremendous guilt regarding the child's death. Her feelings were denied, however, and she immediately became pregnant with Timmy. All the pain, grief, anger, guilt and helplessness of the first child's death landed squarely on Timmy's shoulders. The parents couldn't separate Timmy from the child who had died. It was as though they were rescuing the dead child over and over again. Timmy, as himself, was never seen.

Too Hot: Victim

Victim "too hot" families are similar in many ways to over-protective families. Much of the parents' history is the same, in that the parents often suffer from extreme losses of their own traumatized pasts. The difference is, however, that in these families, the children are expected to give their lives for the victimized parent. The key words to this family might be, "You'll never suffer as I have suffered. Your emotions, behaviors and attempts at independence are selfish. You owe me."

The parents or adult caretakers behave like victims to either their acknowledged or unacknowledged pasts. The children in these families are not only in charge of their parents' moods and happiness, but also experience them as "too soft." The children have little to push up against. They learn that their emotions can topple a full grown giant. The children, therefore, grow up feeling enormous shame and guilt for experiencing normal emotions. The adult caretakers experience depressions, constant worry to the point of panic, phobias and fear of the outside world. They over-react to almost everything, and cling to their children for support, shaming them for their needs.

Typically, children in "too hot" victim families experience debilitating shame for needs and emotions. They also suffer enormous shame and survival guilt when they are successful or happy in their lives. Many destroy their own successes, unconsciously feeling that they have no right to pleasure because their parents are so miserable. They tend to be hypersensitive to the needs of others and feel tremendous guilt when those around them are not happy.

"Too Hard" Families

Children in "too hard" families are often reared by parents who are enormously strict and abusive, treating normal childhood behavior as enormous violations. Or the adult caretakers are "too soft" and the child feels terrified of the injury that normal emotions can cause others. Many families are extremely inconsistent, bouncing between extreme strictness and neglectful permissiveness. In all cases it is the child's self that is attacked rather than merely her or his behavior.

"Too Cold" Families

Children who grow up in "too cold" families not only share the same experiences of debilitating shame and guilt, but also have a great deal more difficulty validating the experience of childhood shame in adulthood. Often their families "looked good" from inside and out. If we were standing at the window looking in, we might see everyone sitting by the fireplace reading a book or viewing a family dinner table set with flowers and candles. Everyone might be eating quietly while one parent or another asks how each child's day went. It might remind us of *Ozzie and Harriet* or *Leave It to Beaver* until we stepped inside. If we were sensitive to tension, we might feel like we were going to explode in all the niceness.

Too Cold: Perfect

Two kinds of "too cold" families I have experienced are the "perfect family" and the "blown-apart family." Perfect, Chameleon and Giant in the first chapter may appear to have the "perfect family." Giant is in the den, Perfect is busily doing her homework and Chameleon is helping her be even more perfect. We might hear words of praise for the assignments she has completed, perhaps seemingly kind words like, "Darling, are you sure you really want to do it that way?" For those who grew up in chaotic families, this might look like the answer to paradise. We know, however, by reading the tale that Perfect lived in high places that were anything but paradise.

Once inside the perfect family, we might pick up messages like, "Don't make waves . . . Make us proud; correct our life. You are what you do . . . Don't let us down . . . You don't want to cause us problems, do you, dear? You are the perfect child and you better stay that way for all our sakes . . . No one is really good enough for you or us . . . Always think of us first . . . What would the neighbors say? Don't get upset, dear . . . Put on a happy face."

A child learns very quickly in the "too cold" perfect family that emotions other than happiness must never be expressed, and even too much happiness may be questionable. They learn not to speak of things that might be distasteful like sexuality, sadness or abuse. Children are shamed for their emotions, their mistakes, their less than perfect body or dress. Shaming, however, is often delivered subtly in gestures, facial expressions, silence, turns of the head or words delivered in a level tone of voice.

In Perfect's case, her mother laughed subtly at unwanted feelings or needs. She might say, "You really don't mean that, dear" or "You have no needs that we have not filled for you, silly girl."

Anger is obviously out of the question, so Perfect learned early to turn anger against herself and experience constant debilitating guilt. Rules in this family are rigid and affection is sparse. Many adults who have begun to work on their feelings of debilitating shame sometimes feel touch starved because there was so little touching in their families.

"What will the neighbors say?" are the most important words spoken and the foundation upon which this family was built. Sometimes, the parents come from families of chaos or families they felt ashamed of for one reason or another. Both parents tend to be shamed-based. Everything but "perfect things" about extended family and others connected with the family is hidden. This family is a family with secrets. Sometimes the generational pain in these families is enormous. There is very little communication other than surface communication. The surface may sound good but there is often a boiling pot of emotions simmering under the mask of stoicism and gaiety. Children in perfect families may even have surgery on parts of their bodies to get rid of even minor facial features that are not perfect. If there is any form of illness, physical or mental, that arises in a family member, or if a family member has been abused, it is rarely talked about.

I once had a friend who grew up in a "perfect family." She developed a progressive illness when we were in college. One of the symptoms was a red blotchy rash that would appear under her eyes and across the bridge of her nose. When her parents came to visit her at the graduate school shortly after her illness was diagnosed, they insisted on taking both of us out to dinner. When I suggested that they might want time with their daughter alone, the mother responded, "Why no, dear. Of course we want you to come along." When my friend would attempt to talk about her feelings, her mother would interrupt, "Yes, honey, I know it's awful but we must make ourselves think of happier things. Just keep your chin up and it will be all right." At one point, one of her parents suggested that she might use a heavier powder to cover the rash.

Too Cold: Blown Apart

Similar to "too cold" perfect families, blown-apart families stifle emotions. These are families of such heavy generational denial of pain that there appears to be almost no communication. Even surface communication is minimal. Painful family secrets are not only hidden, they are denied.

There is extreme emphasis on good behavior, mostly behavior that will keep everybody out of everybody's way.

As adults, children in these families report feeling numb almost from birth. They have many physical illnesses and a great deal of difficulty in relationships.

Adult children from "too cold" blown-apart families report that they don't know their parents at all and often felt they were merely pieces of furniture in the house when they were growing up. These families often refuse to recognize trauma or even physical illness. The major link between the children and their parents is a financial one. They typically feel ashamed of their very existence and sometimes focus on work and finances because the major way love is shown in this "too cold" family is through money. Some children become compulsive spenders and workaholics. Some feel tremendous shame about purchasing anything because, "I obviously didn't need it."

The compulsion to shoplift and steal from one's parents in these families is often a way to "steal" love and nurturing. The families are actually "blown apart" by generational pain and the debilitating shame of all members.

The foregoing examples are only symptomatic of "too hot," "too cold," "too soft" and "too hard" families. Many families that are shame-based are combinations of the different types at different life cycles of the family.

When children grow up and leave these families, they, like Goldilocks, set out on a search for "just right." Many of us made promises very early in our lives not to be like Mom or Dad or our grandparents or other adult caretakers. We find, however, even with the best of intentions and perseverance, we may have recreated another shame-based family, which may not be exactly the same but possesses similar ghosts.

When an adult child has been raised in a chaotic "too hot" family, they may promise themselves that *their* family is going to be happy. But without recovery from debilitating shame and the development of new skills in relationships, this adult will have difficulty feeling intimacy. They may devote all their time to their children, yet have difficulty setting limits and following through because of the pain they experience every time their child cries. The child's tears tug at their own uncried tears and they will do anything to make the child happy again. In order for the child to feel safe, they may have to act out more in order to get the external limits they need for healthy growth. The child's acting-out may create chaos in the family. The child ends up feeling too powerful and acts out the parents' unresolved anger and tears.

Ironically every human being strives for health from birth to death. We don't set out to repeat legacies of debilitating shame and guilt in our children. The part of the process that is often ignored when we set off to find "just right" is the healing of ourselves. "Just right" isn't out there somewhere, it's deep inside ourselves. Healing involves giving a voice to our own hurt child of the past, a voice that we need to hear in order to heal.

Conclusion

An Honest Lullaby

A number of years ago when I was driving home from work, I heard a song playing on the radio. The words struck something inside me so I turned up the volume. It was a song by Joan Baez called "An Honest Lullaby." The words that caught my attention were, "I look around and I wonder how the years and I survived. I must have had a mother that sang to me an honest lullaby."

I found myself singing the words over and over again for the next several days. I realized that children who grow up with debilitating shame never had anyone to sing that honest lullaby.

Shame is an isolating feeling. We keep it hidden. Yet the more we isolate it, hiding it behind the masks that were once demanded of us, the bigger it grows and the lonelier we feel. The more shame we feel, the more internal anger we feel. The greater the anger, the greater the fear of abandonment. We may express the anger or turn it back on ourselves in the form of depression. We feel guilty in an attempt to save our attachment to others. Then, of course, we feel shame all over again.

Feeling forced to live behind a mask of a once considered acceptable self is debilitating. It is also a double bind. If we let ourselves and others see and hear our shameful secrets, we fear abandonment. If we don't, our shame increases and we can never feel fully accepted or loved by others. Of even more importance, we cannot fully love and honor ourselves.

I wish I could say that there is a magical solution to recovery from debilitating shame but I cannot. Unlike fairy tales, human pain has no magical solutions. The good news is that stages of recovery are not difficult to understand. Making a connection regarding the shame with another human being is the first step in recovery. Yet, when one's life has been shame-based, connecting with another about shame feels very risky.

When our lives have been based on the deeply felt internal belief that the only way to survive is to selectively disown parts of ourselves, it is difficult to trust enough to begin to uncover those disowned parts. An individual suffering from sexual abuse, for instance, feels that to share the abuse history with a partner means certain rejection. Indeed, to hear oneself say the words out loud is terrifying. Acknowledging to another means self-acknowledgement. Self-acknowledgement requires us to feel not only the pain of the shameful emotion, its characteristics or behaviors, but also the dimensions of the mask that we have hidden behind for a lifetime. Once we have seen the mask and explored the pain under it, it is hard to wear it in the same way again. When a person who has been forced to hide behind a mask of being perfect and very, very good tells someone about a history of shoplifting, it's terrifying. He or she might wonder if they can ever be seen, or see themselves as Perfect again. When Perfect shared her anger and feelings of being average for the first time or even allowed Human Being to see the stupid child she thought she was, it felt momentarily devastating. When Human Being supported her and validated her pain, she felt a real connection with another for the first time. The shame was then relieved. It would be difficult once she felt and shared her imperfections to wear again the "perfect" mask. By that time, however, Perfect didn't feel the need to cover herself as she once had.

Facing shame also means grieving the loss of the fantasy adult who raised us and separating from their fantasy person internally. It may mean seeing the real adult as they are for the first time. It means accepting ourselves as autonomous.

When one experiences debilitating shame throughout childhood, trust for self and others is jeopardized or destroyed. It takes a great deal of time with another to trust them enough, or more accurately, trust oneself with them enough, to share the shame. Trust involves testing.

Perfect uncovered her shame a little bit at a time. At first, she was only comfortable in tall grasses. If Human Being had laughed at her, judged her, been silent or turned away, she wouldn't have been able to gradually share more. He asked her questions, listened, was empathetic and didn't turn away from her pain. Some of us, however, don't find healthy "human beings" the first time we share deeply felt hidden parts of ourselves. The defensiveness, coldness, or judgment we receive from those who are not in their own recovery from shame may increase our shame. Sometimes it reinforces our belief that we can't trust ourselves and others. We may temporarily increase the protection of our vulnerable self at all costs. We may cover our wounds with more layers and masks. We might ignore ourselves and again adapt to the requirements of others.

It is important not to re-shame ourselves in the process of our recovery. The wounded child inside us doesn't need more injury. We need to accept our own pacing and give ourselves the right to test others before sharing our shame. We can then slowly begin to sing ourselves an honest lullaby. We need to start turning down the volume on those ghosts from the past. We need to be aware of any shaming from those who are currently in our lives, then take the hand of the wounded child inside us and lead her or him away. Above all, we need to begin to be aware when we are shaming ourselves.

Helen Lynd said it well in her book, *On Shame and the Search for Identity*, "The very fact that shame is an isolating experience also means that if one can find ways of sharing and communicating it, this communication can bring about closeness with other persons and with other groups." (Lynd, p. 66)

When I was a child in a shaming family, I used to blame myself when others emotionally kicked me. I would try to figure out what was wrong with me and change myself accordingly. When I was early in my awareness of my shame-based history and was emotionally kicked, I would try to figure out why the other was injuring me. Later in the process, when emotionally kicked, I would seek out others who felt as wounded as I was. Now when I'm emotionally kicked, I tell the kicker to stop and if they won't, I remove myself from their proximity. Then I seek out those I love and who in turn love me so that I can share my feelings and ask for comfort.

Bibliography

Baez, Joan. An Honest Lullaby, 1979.

Baum. **The Wonderful Wizard of Oz**. G.M. Hill, 1900.

Bowlby, John. **Attachment and Loss,** Vol. I, "Attachment." New York: Basic Books, 1969.

Bowlby, John. **A Secure Base: Parent-Child Attachment and Healthy Human Development.** New York: Basic Books, 1988.

Bradshaw, John. **Bradshaw On: Healing The Shame That Binds You.** Deerfield Beach, Florida: Health Communications, 1988.

Cashden, Sheldon. **Object Relations Therapy: Using the Relationship.** New York: W. W. Norton & Company, Inc., 1988.

Crisp, Polly. "Projective Identification: Clarification in Relation to Object Choice," Vol. 5, Number 4, *Psychoanalytic Psychology*. Hillside, New Jersey: Lawrence Erlbaum Associates, Publishers, 1988.

Disney, Walt. **Snow White and the Seven Dwarfs,** 1956.

Elkind, David. **The Hurried Child: Growing Up Too Fast Too Soon.** Reading: Addison-Wesley, 1988.

Fossum, Merle and Mason, Marilyn. **Facing Shame, In Families Of Recovery.** New York: W. W. Norton, 1986.

Freeman, Lucy and Strean, Herbert S. **Guilt — Letting Go.** New York: John Wiley, 1986.

Freud, Sigmund. **The Ego and the Id,** London: Hogarth Press, 1957.

Fromm, Erich. **The Art of Loving.** New York: Harper & Brothers, 1956.

Gruen, Arno. **The Betrayal of the Self, The Fear of Autonomy in Men and Women.** New York: Grove Press, 1988.

Kagan, Richard and Schlosberg, Shirley. **Families in Perpetual Crisis.** New York: W. W. Norton, 1989.

Kaufman, Gershen. **Shame, The Power of Caring.** Cambridge, Massachusetts: Schenkman, 1980.

Klein, M. "Some Theoretical Conclusions Regarding the Emotional Life of the Infant." In M. Klein (ed), (1975). **Envy and Gratitude and Other Works,** 1946-1963. New York: Delacorte Press, 1952.

Klein, M. and Tribich, D. "Kernberg's Object-Relations Theory: A Critical Evaluation." *Int. J. Psychoanalysis*, 62, 27-43, 1981.

Lerner, Harriet Goldbor, Ph.D. **The Dance of Intimacy.** New York: Harper & Row, 1989.

Lewis, Helen Block. **The Role of Shame in Symptoms Formation.** Hillside, New Jersey: Lawrence Erlbaum, 1987.

Lynd, Helen Merrell. **On Shame and the Search for Identity.** New York: Science Editions, 1958.

Middelton-Moz, Jane, **Children Of Trauma, Rediscovering Your Discarded Self.** Deerfield Beach, Florida: Health Communications, 1989.

Middelton-Moz, Jane and Dwinell, Lorie. **After the Tears, Reclaiming the Personal Losses of Childhood.** Pompano Beach, Florida: Health Communications, 1986.

Miller, Alice. **The Drama of the Gifted Child.** New York: Basic Books, 1981.

Minuchin, Salvador; Rosmen, Bernice L. and Baker, Lester. **Psychosomatic Families, Anorexia Nervosa in Content.** Cambridge, Massachusetts: Harvard University Press, 1978.

Peterson, C.; Schwartz S., and Seligman, M.E.P. "Self-Blame and Depressive Symptoms." *Journal of Personality and Social Psychology*, 42, 1981, 253-258.

Richardson, Dr. Ronald W. **Family Ties that Bind.** Vancouver, Canada: International Self-Counsel Press, 1984.

Woititz, Janet Geringer. **Adult Children of Alcoholics.** Pompano Beach, Florida: Health Communications, 1983.